IRELAND IN TRANSITION

Ireland in Transition

Edited by

Kieran A. Kennedy

The Thomas Davis Lecture Series
General Editor: Michael Littleton

Published in collaboration with
Radio Telefís Éireann
by
THE MERCIER PRESS
CORK and DUBLIN

The Mercier Press Limited
4 Bridge Street, Cork
24 Lower Abbey Street, Dublin 1

Ireland in Transition
First Published 1986

Ireland in Transition:
  economic and social change since 1960.
  —(The Thomas Davis lecture series)
  1. Ireland—Social conditions
  I. Kennedy, Kieran A.   II. Radio Telefís Éireann
  III. Series
  941.70824   HN400.3.A8

ISBN 0-85342-786-0

Typeset by Alphaset, Limerick.
Printed by Litho Press Co. Ltd., Midleton, Co. Cork.

The Thomas Davis Lectures
General Editor: Michael Littleton
Every autumn, winter and spring since September 1953, Radio Telefís Éireann has been broadcasting half-hour lectures, named in honour of Thomas Davis. Inspired by one of his famous sayings, 'Educate that you may be free', the aim of these lectures has been to provide in popular form what is best in Irish scholarship and the sciences.

  Most of the lectures have been in series; many have been single broadcasts; some have been in English; some in Irish. In the time that has passed since they were initiated the lectures have dealt with many aspects and with many centuries of Irish social life, history, science and literature. The lecturers, distinguished for their special learning at home and abroad, have been drawn from many nations but mainly from Ireland.

Contents

Foreword

That eminent historian, Professor Oliver MacDonagh, may find it somewhat incongruous that the twenty-fifth anniversary of The Economic and Social Research Institute should be commemorated by a series of Thomas Davis Lectures. 'Was not', he might ask, 'the economic development of Ireland anathema to Davis who assumed that it must necessarily mean importing to Ireland the dark Satanic mills of the Industrial Revolution that he detested so much?'

Davis' ideal Ireland has been described as a paradise of peasant land-owners, high-minded scholars and ecumenical saints. But this was only part of his ambivalence. After a visit to Germany in 1839 he returned an enthusiastic convert to German romanticism. Ireland, he believed, should follow the example of Prussia whose genius had successfully resisted the French both militarily and culturally. In Professor MacDonagh's view, 'Davis' conventional radicalism slipped away, to be replaced by the German romantic's assumption that national culture, national history and national language were not merely ornamental, but integral to national identity'. In Ireland's case the culture to be rejected was English not French.

MacDonagh is inclined to think that Davis and his journal, the *Nation,* were indulging in mere lip-service when they extolled Sir Robert Kane who severely insisted that natural industrial, mineral and maritime resources would have to be developed if Ireland were to become a modern state. MacDonagh maintains that the *Nation* idealised the peasant and identified anglicisation with urbanisation, commercialism and mechanisation. He suggests that the model of a modern state for Davis and the *Nation* was 'indefinite and amateurish, without any understanding or perhaps knowledge of modern science, technology or manufacturing process or organisation'. This, indeed, is a harsh judgement. Davis and his colleagues, it should be remembered, were writers and lawyers appealing to those Irish men and women whom they saw paralysed in a cultural swamp; they were thinkers and propagandists, not scientists or technocrats, and their recognition of Sir Robert Kane shows that they were not exclusively 'racy of the soil'.

The prospectus of the *Nation,* drafted by Thomas Davis in 1842, declared in its second paragraph: 'The liberal journals of Ireland were perhaps never more ably conducted than at this moment; but their tone and spirit are not of the present, but the past; their energies are shackled by old habits, old prejudices, and old divisions; and they do not and cannot keep in the van of the advancing people'.

It was this aspect of Davis that led another outstanding historian, the late Professor T.W. Moody, as a member of the Radio Éireann Council, to suggest in 1953 that Radio Éireann should annually broadcast a series of talks designed to reflect the best in contemporary Irish scholarship in a form that lay listeners could understand. The title of the series derived from Davis' precept 'Educate that you may be free'. The first lecture was broadcast on 27 September 1953 appropriately by the late Dr Myles Dillon, a grandson of a founder of the *Nation,* initiating a series on early Irish society. There have been lectures every winter since then on subjects including Irish literature, history and science by scholars of unquestionable authority and subsequently published in book form.

Ireland in Transition, therefore, fits easily under the rubric that Moody had borrowed from Davis — 'Educate that you may be free'. MacDonagh is right, of course, to remind us of Davis' horror of the evils of the early Industrial Revolution. But the founders of the *Nation* would surely have acclaimed the work of an Institute whose distinctive objective is, to quote its director, 'to address itself to the more important social and economic problems, rather than the minor side-issues that often engage the attention of academics. But while the Institute's research is intended to be practical and useful, it nevertheless tries to bring to bear the best academic theories and knowledge on the problems is confronts'. Similarly, Davis would have welcomed the Institute's procedures in having all its main studies sent for the approval of expert external referees before publication.

I have little doubt that Davis would have nodded approval to many of the lectures in *Ireland in Transition* and listened with delight to more than a few of them. Indeed, some would have evoked memories of writings in his own *Nation* — 'Ireland in the World Economy', 'Employment, Unemployment and Emigration',

'Crime and the Criminal Justice System' and 'Wither Ireland? the next Twenty-five Years', to select but a few. And I am certain that he would enthuse with his friends, John Blake Dillon and O'Neill Daunt over Finola Kennedy's strikingly original lecture 'The Family in Transition'. Of course; it is invidious to name a few lectures from a collection of such variety and consistently high standard; I do so to demonstrate to my friend Oliver MacDonagh some of the more tangible links between this publication and the *Nation* and between Thomas Davis and the work of the Institute. It is, indeed, gratifying that most of the contributors are, or have been, associated with the Institute either as staff or members of the Council. We are glad that Radio Telefís Éireann found the lectures appropriate to a series of such prestige; our director, Kieran A. Kennedy, had a most demanding task as consulting editor, and he discharged it with his accustomed energy and distinction; and we are indebted to Michael Littleton for his guidance and enthusiasm as producer of the series.

Patrick Lynch
Chairman, The Economic and Social Research Institute

1. Economic Development
1958-1985

T.K. Whitaker

Twenty-five years ago I gladly played a part in bringing The Economic Research Institute into being. On the basis of a grant obtained from the Ford Foundation of $280,000, equivalent at the time to £100,000, the Institute kept going for five years and then, as originally agreed, public funding took over. In 1966 the scope of the Institute's research was enlarged to include social topics and it became The Economic and Social Research Institute. The staff was increased but it is mainly the ravages of inflation that have raised running costs from an incredibly low £20,000 a year average of the first five years to the £1 million a year now required. That £1 million would, in 1960 money, be less than £100,000, a homely illustration of one of the most significant — and almost universal — experience of much of the past twenty-five years, namely, high inflation.

Just before the Institute came on stage a more auspicious scene had been set by documents published in 1958 which gave economic policy a new direction and impetus and generated hope of steadier and less sluggish national development. Domestic re-adjustments, particularly the gradual dismantling of protection and the encouragement of industrial investment in Ireland by foreign firms, were helped by the buoyancy of world trade and an atmosphere of confidence and optimism throughout the western world. I shall be describing briefly in a moment the economic and social advances achieved in Ireland during the 1960s. This may help to explain why this decade, though the glamour was beginning to wear off towards the end, has come in retrospect to be regarded nostalgically as a sort of Paradise Lost.

First, however, let us take a quick backward look at our Pilgrim's Progress over the first thirty-five years or so of our existence as an independent state. Progress was beset by many problems and had been painfully slow. The first decade was clouded by civil war and then preoccupied with reconstruction, though not so exclusively as to deny state enterprise its great achievement in harnessing the power of the River Shannon. It is, incidentally, an interesting reflection that the electricity station then criticised as being likely to exceed national needs for many years now contributes less than 4% of those needs. The second decade brought us through a world depression, and the so-called 'economic war' with Britain, into the Second World War, admittedly leaving us better prepared to endure that emergency because of the industries which had risen up behind a generous and indiscriminate tariff screen. Scarcity conditions persisted for years after the war and in the 1950s serious balance of payments deficits rocked the economy. These deficits, which ate into the sterling we had been forced to save in two world wars, were partly the effect of domestic expansionary policies but reflected more fundamentally the danger of relying on agricultural exports as the predominant source of foreign earnings when such supports had to be consigned to one market — the British — where the policy was to keep food prices as low as possible and use cleverly chosen devices, such as deficiency payments, to boost the incomes of British farmers.

Before the scene was changed in the late 1950s, a general mood of despondency prevailed. Economic growth had been so slow and erratic, so many vicissitudes had been encountered, so much population lost by emigration, so few new jobs created in relation to need, that the community was experiencing a dark night of the soul in which doubts were prevalent as to whether the achievement of political independence had not been futile. But at least some lessons had been learned, in particular, the lesson that the pursuit of self-sufficiency, through policies which fostered inefficiency, offered no prospect of employment in Ireland at an acceptable income for those who sought it as an escape from a miserable subsistence on their parents' or a brother's farm. Nor did it provide any assurance of a livelihood, otherwise than by emigration, for the young school-leavers of the towns and cities.

The change of policy in the late 1950s was essentially a recognition of the following four points;

1. Protected manufacture for a home market of dwindling population and low purchasing power gave no hope of *increased* employment.
2. In an increasingly competitive world, in which real wages would

be rising, continued high protection could not guarantee even
the maintenance of existing employment in Ireland at *acceptable*
real wages.

3. If employment were to be created for the fresh thousands seeking work every year — indeed even if existing jobs were to be
safe-guarded — industry must quickly become more efficient so
that its products could be sold on an increasing scale in export
markets.

4. The most effective and advantageous way of achieving the rapid
and general increase required in industrial efficiency was to
accept a commitment to reduce tariffs in return for external market gains and internal aids and incentives towards modernisa-
tion.

The new departure of 1958 involved the abandonment of a pro-
tectionism that had served its purpose and was now out-moded. At
last it seemed more sensible to attract foreign industry here rather
than watch tens of thousands of young persons leave Ireland every
year to work for the multinationals overseas. Not only was the
development of grassland and its products put before protected
home production of wheat — grass before grain in agricultural policy
— but on the industrial side, export-oriented expansion, even if
under foreign ownership, was preferred to total dependence on
heavily protected and often inefficient concentration on a limited
home market. The place of protection in development policy was
taken by a more coherent and purposeful expansionism, backed by
rising government capital expenditure, a shift towards product public investment, and a strong private capital inflow. During the 1960s
national output grew by over 4% per annum on average, more than
double the previous rate. Tourism prospered. Emigration abated
and by 1966 the population had risen 66,000 above the lowest ever
level of 2.8 million recorded in 1961. It looked as if full employment
might be attainable. For most of the decade this unprecedented performance was achieved without any major balance of payments
trouble and with only a moderate rise in prices. As has been said by
Kieran Kennedy, the director of the ESRI, we were enjoying a 'vir-
tuous circle of growth'.

The most significant difference between now and then is that, in
the 1960s, we were living within our means, and using our own and
external capital to increase those means, whereas today we are liv-

ing beyond our means and are still borrowing heavily abroad to maintain our consumption standards rather than to enable us to produce and earn more. At the start of the 1960s we still had some of the sterling assets accumulated as forced savings in two world wars. During the 1960s most of the external capital we imported came in the form of voluntary investment by foreigners in industrial enterprises and in stocks and shares. At the end of the 1960s we owed only about £100 million in foreign debt incurred by the government or state agencies, as against £11,000 million, today.

The good years were eventually brought to an end by unfavourable developments, domestic and external. Already in the late 1960s there were ominous signs of deterioration. Internationally, inflation gathered pace. The annual price rise of 3% or so to which we had become accustomed moved sharply up to an annual average of 8% for the years 1968-1972. A variety of difficulties threatened the long-sustained momentum of economic growth. The planning process itself came under fire. Programmes were said to have failed because they did not yield automatically results which had been specified as being dependent on the realisation of certain conditions. Only the First Programme emerged unscathed with a success beyond the modest original predictions. The Second, more ambitious and more detailed, ran into difficulties towards the end which tended to shadow its satisfactory overall achievement. The Third ran into the inflation of the turn of the decade. A disenchantment with planning, going beyond reasonable bounds, set in. Despite explicit warnings, frequently repeated, about the conditionality of a plan, its dependence on the validity of the underlying assumptions, and its exposure to disruption from unruly forces both internal and external, people tended to invest a plan with a kind of magic, self-fulfilling automaticity, requiring no support or restraint on their part. Expectations were fuelled by the unprecedented rate of progress achieved over most of the 1960s. In an extremely competitive political environment (there have been six changes of government since 1960) ambitious ministers jibbed at being kept prisoners of a plan and cut free with novel and expensive initiatives. Trade unions favoured planning of everything except wages, the crucial factor in cost competitiveness. While we were discovering all this about plans — and human nature — and were temporarily buoyed up by the excitement of entering the EEC in January, 1973, a totally unexpected disruption was on the way. Towards the end of that year, the price of oil was quadrupled and the world economy plunged into disorder and depression.

Such a big jump in the price of energy could not but force a contraction of spending on other things no matter how quickly and desperately economies in oil consumption were achieved. There was danger in oil-importing countries of extremely depressing effects on living standards and employment, effects which might be accentuated unnecessarily by beggar-my-neighbour policies. Doubtless with the good intention of giving time for a co-ordinated rather than a panic adjustment to the inevitable, various international bodies advised against allowing the oil crisis to exert an uncontrolled deflationary effect. This advice, however, was widely interpreted as 'carry on as before: pretend nothing has happened' and major international banks were ready to 'recycle' the Arab dollars, recycling being, of course, a euphemism for lending countries the money to buy more dear oil than they could really afford. The Central Bank was something of a lone voice in warning that it was not possible for life to go on just as before after such a major increase in energy costs and in stressing that external borrowing should be regarded only as a temporary respite, to give time for basic re-adjustments, and should be devoted to capital purposes rather than the financing of everyday needs.

Most regrettably, however, one defence against excessive financial laxity had been unwisely and unnecessarily thrown down before the oil crisis supervened. In 1972 the convention of not running a deficit in the current budget was deliberately abandoned. The door was, therefore, open in principle in 1974 and later years for recourse to borrowing on a vast scale to meet current expenses: the aggregate current deficit incurred from 1973 to 1977 was nearly £750 million, much of it financed by foreign borrowing. A recent ESRI study has drawn attention to the longer-term ineffectiveness of the expansionary budgets of the 1970s. It is true that a return of more realistic budgeting was heralded in 1977, with tax concessions and investment in job creation traded for a moderate pay agreement, but, in the general election which followed, a new government swept into power committed to a political manifesto and ancillary economic programmes of irrational optimism involving much higher current deficits than ever before. There was no need for so much artificial boosting of economic activity with borrowed money because internal and external conditions were favourable to growth until the second oil crisis occurred at the end of 1979. By then we had already been so misusing our borrowing potential that we had little leeway for stimulating the economy when genuine need arose.

From 1980 to date the story continues of heavy deficits in current budgets and a rapid accumulation of foreign indebtedness. Every person now at work effectively owes £10,000 to foreign lenders. Individuals and groups who worry vociferously about our sovereignty rarely have a word to say about the insidious and real threat to economic independence posed by ever-increasing foreign indebtedness. Even senior politicians indulge in contemptuous references to 'pre-occupation with book-keeping'. If the debt were being incurred to raise national productivity or to create useful additions to national capital in the form, say, of better roads, it could be justified within reasonable limits. But it is otherwise where everyday expenses take all or most of it.

A commitment to reform of this dangerous financial imbalance has marked government declarations for some years past. Such a commitment appeared in the Fianna Fáil plan, *The Way Forward,* published in October, 1982 and prior to publication last year of the present Coalition government's plan, *Building on Reality,* the elimination of the budget deficit by 1987 had been the stated policy. This is now superseded by the much less stringent aim of restricting the deficit to 5% of GNP by that time. This year, however, the deficit is being allowed to rise to about 8% of GNP. Remembering that such single-figure percentages hide actual figures of well over £1,000 million a year, that 60% of current public expenditure relates to pay, pensions and debt service, that much of the rest, including expenditure on social welfare and security, is even more difficult to curtail, and that hopes of a general tax relief are not being totally discouraged, it is difficult to bring oneself to believe that there is a realistic commitment even to a significant reduction of the deficit. The objective of elimination, if not formally abandoned, seems to have been postponed *sine die.* Procrastination, however, merely piles up the agony for the future, increasing the risk that solutions will be imposed from outside rather than chosen by ourselves.

It is a regrettable paradox that, although there is an overwhelming majority in the Dáil of elected representatives sharing a responsible concern for the nation's welfare, their almost equal division into opposing groups tends to neutralise their influence in favour of orthodoxy and to allow disproportionate sway to a small and less

responsible minority. When conditions are so critical it is a great
pity that the major parties have not an agreed commitment to a
basic programme of economic and financial reform. Democracy has
also suffered much in recent years from the habit of powerful
interest groups of declaring their rejection of decisions of government and parliament. No sooner is a tax or local charge enacted, for
instance, than some such group refuses to pay it; no sooner is some
improvement in pay of services denied because it cannot be
afforded than disruption is threatened.

The years since 1973, which have seen such a grave deterioration
in our public finances, have also unfortunately seen unemployment
rise from 66,000 to over 230,000. Within the EEC, however, Irish
agriculture is more surely — if no longer liberally — supported than
in the old days of dependence on the British market. Industrial
exports, mostly from the newer technically advanced firms, are
increasing at a fast rate. The traditional trade deficit has recently
turned into a trade surplus, but this is not yet soundly established
and higher growth and spending will call for higher imports. We
used to have a substantial net income from abroad in the form of
dividends on investments and emigrants' remittances and this
helped to cover our trade deficit. Now it is the other way round. In
spite of receiving hundreds of millions of pounds annually from the
EEC and having a big income from tourism, the net flow on the non-
trade side is outwards. This is due particularly to interest payments
on our foreign debt and the repatriation of profits by external investors. There still remains a substantial current account deficit in the
balance of payments, a crucial measure of the extent to which the
community is living beyond its means. The cause of this is not far to
seek: the blame rests squarely with public sector borrowing which,
unlike private borrowing, can continue on a vast scale for too long
for unproductive purposes. Until this external payments deficit is
reduced and we can truthfully say that what remains boosts productive investment rather than consumption, we will not have a stable
base for further progress.

The financial policy mistakes of the past were grievous and cannot easily be rectified. To borrow more would be to plunge deeper
into the morass. To deflate the economy would make unemployment even worse. The only way out is by careful and sustained
promotion of economic growth. This is a more dynamic and attractive aim than fiscal rectitude, but greater rectitude there must be,

too. Current public expenditure can most effectively be curbed by controlling outlay on public sector pay (which has been done with a good deal of success since 1982) and by being extremely stingy about undertaking *new* expenditure. Capital expenditure that generates losses rather than gains must be weeded out. Better value for money must be insisted upon in all public outlay. In social welfare, universal provision must give way to meeting identified need at least cost. It is by favouring productive investment and encouraging everyone to earn more that policy can best contribute to raising national output. Once the economy has moved to a higher growth path, revenue buoyancy will do much to reduce the current budget deficit provided expenditure is kept in check. But revenue is at present so deficient that no general concessions are possible, at best only relief at the margin in personal taxation. This must be accompanied by continued pay restraint and improved competitiveness. Industrial policy needs to be focused on improving quality, design and added-value. We need to built up large export-oriented indigenous firms, to extend the domestic linkages of foreign firms, to maximise the potential of small industries and to develop exports of services.

The kind of strategy I have just outlined requires a sustained period of discipline during which results will be slow to appear. It is not very appealing to politicians sensitive to frequent tests of public opinion. Yet I cannot see any other valid course.

In the context of a progressive reduction of the current budget deficit and the elimination of wasteful capital expenditure, there would be scope for greater attention to basic infrastructural needs, to the benefit of employment and the whole economy. I have for years been lamenting the lack of organisational capacity which causes us to pay hundreds of millions of pounds in unemployment relief in a country still poorly provided with basic amenities but rich in dilapidation and disrepair. I have suggested how, by using the competitive contract idea, useful community assets might be cheaply and efficiently created to compensate for the excess of normal pay over unemployment relief. Indeed, the contract idea might replace the employee relationship in various work contexts to the advantage of economy, efficiency and industrial relations.

Not only in the 1960s, but in the troubled 1970s as well, living standards were raised but they have been virtually static so far in the 1980s at a level which is still being propped up by foreign borrowing. We need quite a high rate of growth to dispense with this prop, set personal and social standards on a rising scale again and generate enough new jobs to start lowering the present high level of unemployment. The first 2% of growth in national output in any year is swallowed up in matching the population and dependency growth and covering various external outlays, including interest on foreign debt. An annual productivity rise of 2% to 3% a year has to be allowed for in estimating the increase in demand needed to produce new jobs. We can, however, expect some outside help in our efforts to achieve faster progress. The boost given by United States deficits to world trade is still strong and, if it wanes, we must, with our EEC partners, try to persuade Germany to sustain European economic activity by spending and buying more, as they can well afford to do. Oil prices seem certain to fall further, giving relief to our balance of payments. Interest rates also may come down. Inflation is no longer a menace. The rather low rate of exchange with sterling and the American dollar favours sales of goods and services; within the EEC any currency realignment is likely to help rather than hinder. This is the time for us to get going again: circumstances will never be completely favourable.

The last twenty-five years were a period of great social as well as economic change. Perhaps the most significant social change, apart from the improvement in living standards and in social provisions of all kinds, is the substantial rise in population — it is now over 3½ million — and the transformation of Ireland from being a mainly rural to being mainly urban society. Emigration ceased to be a drain on population in the early 1960s and was replaced for quite a while by immigration. At present emigration has resumed but will not stop the population increase as it is much less than the rate of natural increase. It affords some easement of the major social problem of unemployment.

Given firm pursuit of remedial policies there is no need to despair. We recognise our problems and efforts are being made — even if not yet fully convincing — to take them in hand. We must not let 'make believe' take the place of realism, as could so easily happen on the way to the next general election. With sustained will and purpose, and clear recognition of the difficulties to be overcome, our small, compact, younger and better educated society has the potential to resume the progress of the 1960s.

2. Ireland in the World Economy

Dermot McAleese

The Irish economy is closely integrated into the world economy. We depend on foreign countries for most of our industrial raw materials and components, for four-fifths of our machinery, for necessities such as oil and coal and luxuries such as tropical fruits and wines. Our dependence on overseas markets is not confined to the exchange of goods. Foreign manufacturing subsidiaries, for example, account for four out of every ten jobs in Irish industry. There is a substantial foreign presence in mining and exploration for hydrocarbons and a small but significant presence in the financial services sector. Irish and external capital markets are also closely linked. The Irish government has borrowed extensively abroad and its foreign debt is still increasing. Private individuals, both resident and non-resident, also move capital in and out of the country in large amounts each year. Irish capital is internationally mobile. So also is Irish labour and, over the past quarter of a century, thousands of Irish people have found employment in Britain, continental Europe and the United States.

The fact of integration is indisputable. The Irish economy of 1985 has properly been described as a small open economy. Openness in this context is another word for integration. Unlike small size which is something *given,* openness is a variable. Through policy decisions — at home and abroad — an economy can become more open or it can decide to become less open. The thrust of Irish economic policy since the founding of the ESRI has been to make the economy more open, in contrast with the quarter century prior to that, from the early 1930s to the mid-1950s, when the objective had been to make the economy more closed, that is less import-dependent, less reliant on foreign capital. This essay is concerned with the dimensions of Ireland's involvement in the world economy, the reasons for the decision to become more integrated in the world economy and the implications of that decision for our economic growth and standard of living.

THE OPENNESS OF THE IRISH ECONOMY:
TRADE, INVESTMENT, DEBT

The Irish economy has become far more *export-oriented* than it was before. Roughly, half of total manufacturing output produced in Ireland is destined for sale outside the country compared with one-tenth in the late 1950s. About two-thirds of the output of Irish farms is sold abroad. Services have also become an increasingly important source of foreign exchange. Tourism has, of course, always been a significant factor. A growing contribution to Irish export activity has been made by firms engaged in construction-related activities and by medical consultancy organisations. Irish building contractors have worked in Africa and Middle Eastern countries on assignments as diverse as building a radar tracking station in Nigeria, office blocks in Zimbabwe and prefabricated housing for airline staff in Bahrain. Companies such as Guinness Peat Aviation have established a leading position in the international aircraft business and 800 Aer Lingus staff in Ireland are engaged in the maintenance of other countries' aircraft.[1]

All this expansion in activity is reflected in the rise in the ratio of exports of goods and services to national output from 25% in 1960 to its 1985 level of 63%. In 1985, roughly £11,000 million worth of goods and service were exported.

The product composition of Irish exports has changed dramatically. Whereas in the 1950s Ireland's exports consisted mostly of primary goods — live animals, unprocessed meat, dairy products — by the early 1980s manufactured goods had accounted for over 60% of total merchandise exports. The cross-Channel live animal trade has virtually disappeared, food exports are receiving a higher degree of processing and upwards of 40% of our manufactured exports fall into the high-technology product category. The tendency towards greater reliance on manufactured goods and a general raising of the level of sophistication of product is characteristic of most semi-industrialised countries as they progress to industrial maturity.

Export markets have become more diversified. The single most significant development has been the reduction in dependence on the British market. At the time of Independence, virtually all Irish exports were sold to the United Kingdom. By 1960, the United Kingdom share had fallen slightly to 75%. But, by 1984, the share had fallen to 34%. The collapse in the United Kingdom share does not mean that exports to the United Kingdom were falling in absolute terms: in fact, they grew steadily right through the period. Rather, it reflected the rapid growth of exports to areas other than the United Kingdom.

These other areas were primarily continental Europe, in particular the EEC countries. The Irish share of total Irish exports rose from 6% in 1960 to 34% in 1984. But countries outside Europe also claimed an important share. Egypt, Nigeria, Iraq and Libya, countries which would scarcely have been noticed in the Irish trade statistics of the 1950s, became important trading partners.

Accompanying this process of increased export-orientation — and an integral part of it — was the growth of *foreign investment activity* in the Irish economy. It is difficult to say for sure what proporation of Irish industry was indigenously owned in 1960 but it was considerably below the present level. Over one-third of the labour force in the Irish manufacturing sector is employed in overseas subsidiaries. Parent firms are mostly American but there is also a strong representation of German, British and continental European investors. Contrary to popular impression, these parent companies are more often than not small rapidly-growing firms just starting into international production rather than large multinationals. Their subsidiaries in Ireland produce mainly for export — and thus have played a predominant role in the diversification of exports — and they produce components or assemble products which tend to be of high quality. Electronics, office equipment, health care, chemicals and pharmaceuticals are the sectors in which they have made a particular mark. Although the most significant element in foreign investment was investment in manufacturing, other sectors also attracted the attention of the overseas investor. Banking, insurance, the hotel industry, bloodstock, agricultural land, mining and hydrocarbon exploration all experienced a significant inflow of overseas funds.

Foreign trade and foreign investment were themes of the 1960s and 1970s. In recent years, another feature of Ireland's integration in the world economy has attracted attention — *the rise in foreign debt*. Official external debt stands at roughly £11,000 million, equivalent to £10,000 per person at work.[2] Ireland managed to effect the major industrial transition of the 1960s without any significant recourse to foreign borrowing. During the 1970s, however, in response to the oil crisis, the Irish government began to borrow although still within manageable proportions. The debt/GNP ratio was 29% in 1976, 27% in 1979 and 34% in 1980. But over the last five years alone, this figure has doubled to its September 1985 level of 70% of GNP.

Integration is a two-way process and, while I have chosen to emphasise the sources of increased foreign exchange obtained from exports, foreign investment and official debt, there were also corresponding outflows. Increases in exports were, inevitably, associated with increases in imports. As output rose, Ireland needed more capital machinery, more raw materials, more oil and coal, more intermediate goods in order to produce it. As Irish incomes increased, we wanted more variety in basic goods and more expensive luxuries, from foreign holidays to motor cars. As protective barriers fell, the ability of Irish producers to meet foreign competition weakened. As the economy grew in prosperity, it was not surprising that Irish firms should look abroad for investment opportunities. This they have done in considerable volume. The Irish multinational is very much alive and well — Smurfits, Waterford Glass, Cement Roadstone, Rohans, James Crean, being familiar names.

Although integration in the world economy has been emphasised, there were also certain developments which involved a degree of disintegration between Ireland and the outside world. The break in the sterling link in 1979, for example, resulted in a break in parity between the Irish pound and the pound sterling and, as a by-product, to the introduction of exchange controls on capital transactions between the Republic and Northern Ireland and the Republic and Britain. The Common Agricultural Policy also led in its own way to various impediments being placed on cross-border trade in agricultural produce. The discovery of natural gas led to disintegration of a sort — by reducing Ireland's dependence on imported energy by some 15 percentage points.

HOW POLICY CHANGES MADE THE IRISH ECONOMY MORE OPEN

The move towards greater integration was the consequence of domestic policy decisions. These decisions were prompted by the realisation that protection had outlived its usefulness and that a rapidly growing world economy, with free trade and currency convertibility the order of the day, held out great prospects for the development of Irish industry and agriculture.

   The change in policy took place over two decades. First came the encouragement of investment, Irish and foreign, in the less developed regions of Ireland. The tax relief schemes for exports followed in the mid-1950s. Unilateral tariff reductions were implemented in 1963 and 1964. The Anglo-Irish Free Trade Area Agreement, which came into effect in 1966, provided for the removal of Irish tariffs on British goods in exchange for improved access to Irish exporters to the United Kingdom market. Membership of the European Community in 1973 marked the culmination of the trade liberalisation policy. It opened up the European market to Irish agricultural exports. It enabled Ireland to benefit from the Common Agricultural Policy and from the Community's regional and social policy. It meant that Ireland could participate fully in the evolution of the Community into a closer union of nations.

   The new trade arrangements involved the removal of Irish protection on imports from the United Kingdom and other EEC countries and participation in the Common Commercial Policy of the Community. This implied that, from 1973, most decisions affecting trade had to be agreed on a joint Community basis. One notable consequence was that Ireland was able to play a constructive part in the three Lomé Agreements arranged between certain African and other less developed countries and the Community. Through a series of policy measures, therefore, Ireland effectively turned away from a policy of development through protection to one of development through exports.

   In return for providing foreigners with improved access to the Irish market, the government expected Irish enterprises to benefit from free and secure access to the rich markets of the United Kingdom and Western Europe. In the case of agriculture, integration was seen as a special boon. Membership of the European Community opened the European market to the Irish farmer and agricultural producers benefited in full from the price support of the CAP. More important still, the Irish government was able to play an active part in the price discussions at Brussels instead of being, as in the past, the passive spectator and reactor to decisions taken elsewhere.

   As far as the industrial sector was concerned, it was recognised that imports would increase and that some domestic producers would be injured. These effects could, however, be compensated by exploitation of export opportunities by existing producers and by the attraction of new industries, domestic and foreign, which would be capable of responding to the advantages of access to the European market. Restrictions on foreign investment, the legacy of the Control of Manufactures Acts of the 1930s, were withdrawn in the late 1950s.

The expected increase in imports did indeed materialise. The removal of protection placed pressure on sections of Irish industry and meant that increased domestic demand was quickly translated into an increased demand for imported goods and services. For the Irish consumer this was generally a favourable development. It meant more attractive prices, more choice and better quality. Workers and owners of industries bearing the brunt of foreign competition saw things differently. There were job losses in the footwear, clothing, furniture, car assembly and textile industries. But, and this is the relevant qualification, there was sufficient growth in employment elsewhere in the economy, up to 1980 at least, to ensure that overall employment increased.

The extent of import penetration has been remarkable. It is still not widely appreciated that imports account for three-quarters of domestic expenditure on clothing and footwear. In 1959, the import share of expenditure on these products was negligible. So also at that time were exports of clothing and footwear whereas now these industries export over two-thirds of their output and rely on the home market for less than one-third. Import penetration affected services as well as merchandise trade. Foreign holidays, for example, once a luxury for the few are now a refuge for the many from the vagaries of the Irish summer.

Foreign investment also responded to the new opportunities. The growth in multinational activity in Ireland was made possible by two factors. First, protection in Europe was falling which meant that a peripheral country like Ireland could be taken seriously as a base from which to export. Second, the Irish government made it clear that it wanted multinational subsidiaries, that these subsidiaries would be welcomed by all sections of the Irish community and that grants and tax incentives were available to foreign investors to supplement the natural competitive advantages of Ireland as a location. The concept behind all this was from an Irish point of view quite simple. Instead of Irish people emigrating to work for manufacturing companies abroad, subsidiaries of these companies were 'emigrating' to provide work for Irish people at home.

Irish policy towards foreign investment was an example of consistent effective policy-making and an outstanding — perhaps the only outstanding— instance of using fiscal policy, over which political independence had given us discretion, to sustained advantage. A clear decision was made to encourage export-oriented foreign subsidiaires in the manufacturing sector. Investment in other sectors of the economy by multinationals was either not encouraged (e.g., the case of land purchase, property, import-substitution industries already serviced by Irish industry) or else was subject to a separate policy regime (e.g., mining and exploration, banking). The policy had a unique ingredient of success. For once, all sections of the Irish community — government, trade unions, professional bodies — pulled together. And the IDA by hard marketing and innovative thinking made sure that the good news got through to the right people. In the process, it acquired a reputation as an Irish industrial development agency of world class.

Encouraged by the new policies, foreign investment came to Ireland to an extent which exceeded the expectations of those formulating policy in 1959. Overseas subsidiaries brought capital, technological and marketing know-how and employment opportunities to towns and villages across the land. Apart from a few well-publicised exceptions, the subsidiaries acted as good citizens and provided well-paid employment and useful experience to thousands of young Irish people. The multinationals provided precisely those attributes which Ireland tended to lack. The Irish were deficient in marketing; overseas subsidiaries arrived with marketing networks already established. Lacking in industrial tradition, the Irish tended to be weak in technical aspects of industry; the multinationals supplied technical know-how. Overseas subsidiaries did not create these weaknesses in Irish industry which are merely a reflection of Ireland's comparatively underdeveloped state. They compensated for them.

INTEGRATION AND FLEXIBILITY

Until about 1980, the policies of freer trade, outward-looking policies and economic integration by and large delivered the promised benefits. 'Freer' rather than 'free' trade is the operative word. The Irish government insisted on a long transition period — ten years in the case of AIFTAA and five in the case of the EEC. Special treatment was afforded to sensitive industries such as motor vehicles and the Common Commercial Policy provided protective shelter to many labour intensive industries from competition from outside the Common Market. Most important of all, by opting for less commodity protection, the Irish government did not entirely abandon the notion of protecting Irish industry. The provision of industrial incentives — capital grants, export profits relief, etc., — involved the replacement of commodity protection with factor-based incentives. In this way, the potentially adverse impact of large tariff reductions in import-competing domestic industry was modified.

The benefits of the new policy were evident in the more specialised and more productive industrial structure and in the rapid industrial growth of the 1960s and 1970s. During the 1980s, however, the economy's performance deteriorated. In part this was the result of a worsening international environment but questions were also asked about whether the move to openness had proceeded too fast and whether, in the drive to attract foreign industry, indigenous firms had received less attention than they merited. There was a whiff of protectionist arguments of the 1930s in the Telesis Report's assertion that no country had succeeded in developing high levels of industrial income without a strong indigenous sector.

The question still remains, however, as to whether Ireland made full use of the opportunities which access to the markets of Europe and membership of the European Community opened up. Our record in this respect is patchy. Irish governments obtained a disproportionate share of the European Social Fund, European Investment Bank loans and agricultural price support moneys. The proportion of American investment in Europe attracted to Ireland was also well above that which could be expected on the basis of population or national income. Yet there were also aspects in which the country was far less successful. One thinks of the comparative failure of indigenous Irish firms to develop markets in continental Europe — a failure which may go back to inadequate language training at school level and insufficient attention to marketing skills at third-level institutions. Irish agriculture also failed to upgrade its output at a sufficiently rapid pace. More generally, the economy failed to develop the degree of flexibility and adaptability which are essential ingredients of success in a small open economy.

The trend in external debt illustrates this point. To some extent, it was the result of Ireland's integration in the world capital market

— this made borrowing easier. As a country with progressive outward-looking policies, a member country of the European Community and politically stable, Ireland was seen as an attractive bor-
rower by a financial world awash with credit in the 1970s. Interest
rates, after allowing for inflation, were much cheaper then than they
are now. The Euopean Community made special funds available
through the European Investment Bank, first to encourage energy
projects and, following membership of the EMS (in 1979), to fund
infrastructural investment. These favourable supply conditions
appeared just at a time when the hold of successive Irish governments' on public expenditure began to weaken disastrously and the
dollar, the currency of denomination of most of the external debt,
began to soar.

Despite the efforts to curb its growth in recent years, the level of
foreign debt continues to increase. A financial journalist described
the economy as 'an international banking anomaly' which has the
largest foreign debt per head in the world — 'yet sharp-suited bankers are still pestering the Department of Finance with offers of
more money'.[3] The difficulty is to know when the bankers will
change from pestering the Department with offers of money to pestering it with demands for repayment!

The spiralling of Ireland's foreign debt has done serious damage
to the economy. The damage is not assessable solely in terms of the
cost of debt service, considerable though that sum evidently is. Ireland's credibility in an international context has tended to be undermined. Prospective foreign investors — direct investors, not financial institutions — must look askance at a nation so deeply in the
red. Political independence does not require economic self-sufficiency — this point was argued forcefully in 1959 by Professor
Lynch in his demolition of the Sinn Féin myth of self-sufficiency as
a goal of economic policy.[4] But some degree of undermining of
political status, neutrality and respect must follow from the high
levels of external debt presently obtaining in the economy.

The weakness of the Irish economy was exposed in the
background documents of the New Ireland Forum Report. The picture painted of the Northern Ireland and the Republic economies
were both unflattering in the extreme. Both economies had slow
growth, high unemployment and were spending substantially more
than they earned. The difference was that the north was being bank-
rolled by *ex gratia* payments from the British Exchequer whereas

the Republic was accumulating debt which would eventually have to be serviced from taxation. The Republic could not on its own make a financial contribution to any proposed constitutional change. A question mark arose as to whether Irish unity would be in the economic interests of Northern Catholics let alone Northern Protestants. Political issues are not, of course, decided on the basis of economic calculus but the fact that the question arises shows how much ground has been lost.

Another instance of opportunities not fully grasped concerned membership of the EMS in 1979. Under this system, the Irish pound's value is fixed, within narrow limits, to the value of the ECU, the ECU consisting of a given amount of member states' currencies. Membership of the EMS meant breaking parity with sterling — the first break since 1826 — and establishing a new foreign exchange regime. Because of the strength of sterling, the EMS did not have the expected effect of reducing Irish inflation in the early years of our entry into the System. It is doubtful if the sterling link would have survived in any event. Clearly it would have been inappropriate for the Irish pound to have followed sterling in its ascent backed up by North Sea oil and the strong monetary policies of Mrs Thatcher.

The EMS gave added impetus to the debate on Irish competitiveness, since cost-competitiveness, under the new regime, could in the short run at least be affected by changes in the exchange rate as much as by changes in domestic cost conditions. To avoid the problem of loss of competitiveness required a higher degree of flexibility of response by income earners and firms to sterling and dollar exchange fluctuations than the economy could deliver. The result has been an unfortunate tendency for Irish labour costs to rise relative to European levels. This has accentuated the unemployment problem. Perhaps it also opened our eyes yet again to the basic truth that foreigners will only buy our goods or come to visit Ireland or set up factories if Irish people offer good value for money. Value for money is not achieved by paying ourselves more for doing exactly the same work as before.

CONCLUSION
First, openness, free trade, the presence of multinationals, is a means of escaping from the restrictions of small size. Outward-looking policies in that sense helped Ireland to become more prosper-

ous. Being more prosperous, we are far better placed to withstand the fluctuations of the world economic climate than if we had remained closed and poor.

Second, the world is becoming more not less interdependent in economic terms. There is no possibility of putting the clock back even if we wanted to. The European Commission is pressing for greater not less integration within the markets of the Community. We can expect over the next decade much greater harmonisation of taxes and openness of market mechanisms.

Third, openness does not mean that the domestic market should be ignored. The domestic market is the seed-bed of future exporters. Sales to the home market provide half of total employment in Irish industry and the loss of the home market to foreign competition has contributed to the rise in unemployment. The idea that people should sell Irish and should check for the availability of Irish goods whenever possible is based on sound economic principles. But the operating principle must be not to keep foreign goods out of the Irish market — which could be applied against us to keep Irish exports out of foreign markets — but to keep Irish goods in. That can be done by making sure that they are competitive.

Fourth, openness is not a formula which guarantees success. There are prosperous small economies such as the Scandanavian countries, Belgium, the Netherlands and Luxembourg, and Far Eastern economies such as Korea and Singapore which have harnessed the benefits of international specialisation and turned them into an engine of growth. There are instances of failure in Eastern Europe and Latin America, where small countries have frittered away the potential gains through bad internal policy decisions and corrupt government. These countries have degenerated to a point where autonomous development has become very difficult.

The general conclusion of this essay is that for a small country to prosper in an unstable and changing world it has to be well-managed economically and it has to be able to adjust quickly. Ireland's experience with outward-looking policies has been broadly successful, first, because the economy was well-managed through most of the period, although it did not necessarily seem so at the time, and second, because the favourable international environment helped to sustain domestic growth and hence made adjustment easier.

During the past decade, however, the position has deteriorated on both fronts. The international economy has slowed down.

Foreign competition for Irish producers' markets has stiffened. There are fewer foreign investment projects around and the IDA has to struggle harder to attract them to Ireland. The tourism industry has been dealt a heavy blow by the violence in Northern Ireland. The British economy, with which our economic welfare is still closely interwoven, has been in relative decline although happily there have been signs of recovery in recent years. The contrast between the world economy's performance in the early 1960s and in the early 1980s could scarcely be greater.

The management of the economy has also suffered setbacks over the past decade. Perhaps the initial success with outward-looking policies made us take this success too much for granted. The task of adjusting to a slower-growing world economy was undertaken belatedly and with reluctance. We underestimated the importance of flexibility in the economy. Flexibility in work practices, flexibility in wages and salaries, flexibility in response to changes in the pattern of international trade. We devoted too much effort to discussion of income distribution and not enough to how income itself would be generated. Symptomatic of that general trend was the rise in social welfare provisions which, from being well below the British level in the early 1970s, have now reached almost the same level. Few people seem to ask whether a country with two-thirds of Britain's standard of living and with two and a half times its debt per capita can really afford such a high level of benefits. Another cause of the slow pace of adjustment was the resistance by the trade unions — particularly those in the public sector — to revised work practices and wage moderation. Strong sectoral pressures were matched in those years by weak central government with a consequent weakening of the coherence of the macroeconomic framework. Foreign capital available at concessional rates was not used effectively.

The Irish economy is now adjusting to a more realistic development pattern. Prospects for the world economy are looking more favourable than they have been for some time. The combination of faster growth abroad and a more competitive-conscious domestic economy will help Ireland to make better use of the free access to the markets of developed countries which the next twenty-five years is likely to witness.

3. Employment, Unemployment and Emigration

J.J. Sexton

In the course of this essay I will be concerned mainly with developments in the Irish labour market over the past twenty-five years, i.e., broadly covering the period from 1960 to 1985.

Before setting out to chart these developments, however, let us dwell for a few moments on the scene immediately prior to the period chosen. The 1950s can be described as representing one of the lowest points in the recent fortunes of the nation. The economy was stagnant and the level of emigration was massive. The outflow between 1951 and 1961 involved a net population loss of some 400,000 — almost one person in eight when expressed in terms of the population levels which prevailed at that time. The great majority of those who emigrated were aged between 15 and 30 years; up to a third of those who were in this age bracket in 1951 had left the country 10 years later. The culmination of this huge outflow was that by 1961 the population of the Republic had reached its lowest ever level — 2.8 million.

The scale of the emigration which occurred, large as it was, did not prevent unemployment from rising substantially. The numbers on the unemployment register increased to nearly 95,000 in 1957. There were demonstrations in the streets and the degree of discontent was sufficient to enable one of the unemployed to gain election to the Dáil. Indeed we had reached such depths of despondency at that stage that some were speculating about the eventual disappearance of the Irish as a race. One will recall, for example, the series of essays *The Vanishing Irish,* edited by Dr. John A. O'Brien.[1]

In the midst of all of this gloom however some events were occurring which were to provide the cornerstone of recovery. The first economic programme was introduced late in the 1950s which, in time, provided a stimulus to economic growth. As a result the economic situation changed dramatically in Ireland from the beginning of the 1960s. The level of employment began to rise; emigration began to decline significantly, to the extent that it was more than offset by the natural increase in the population (births less deaths) and we entered a phase of significant and sustained population growth.

The industrial sector was very much to the forefront in contributing to expansion during this period. The incentives provided in the way of capital grants, and the generally more vibrant economic atmosphere, stimulated domestic enterprise and attracted many new firms from abroad. The degree of job creation was more than sufficient to offset the decline in the numbers on the land and for the first time in generations a sustained increase in overall employment was achieved. Unemployment fell to quite low levels in the 1960s, partly as a result of progress on the job front but also because the pressure on the labour market was reduced according as greater numbers were accommodated in the educational sector, particularly after the introduction of free secondary education in 1967.

Economic expansion continued on into the 1970s and the general expectation at the beginning of that decade was one of considerable optimism. There had been vicissitudes, of course, such as in 1966 and 1970, but in retrospect these were mere hiccups when compared with the economic onslaughts which we have had to face in more recent years.

The early 1970s saw another significant watershed in population terms. Even though some young people continued to emigrate, they were outnumbered by the return of older former emigrants and their families. We were remarkably in a situation of immigration not emigration. This created a minor population explosion; in the ten years after 1971 the population of the Republic rose by nearly half a million to over 3.4 million, which meant that by 1981 it had regained the level which prevailed in or about 1890.

The pace of employment expansion was brought to a temporary halt in 1974 when we began to feel the full impact of the deep world-wide recession which followed the oil crisis of October 1973. The combined effect of this contraction in employment with the continuing growth in the numbers available for work caused unemployment to reach then unprecedented heights — about 110,000 at the height of that recession.

However, the recessionary forces receded after 1976 and this, combined with the effect of expansionary policies set in train when the new Fianna Fáil government assumed office in 1977, gave rise to a sharp but short explosion in employment. Between 1977 and 1979 the numbers at work in Ireland rose by over 60,000; unemployment fell but the continuing pressure of population and labour force growth was such that the jobless total could not be brought back to the level which existed before the mid-decade recession.

The employment gains of the late 1970s were however bought at a price. The expansion in the economy was achieved by means of substantial tax concessions and increased public expenditure which were increasingly sustained by foreign borrowing. Higher personal expenditure sucked in more imports and the balance of payments position deteriorated. When the world economy went into deep recession again following the second oil price shock of 1979 the scope for taking corrective measures was restricted. We, as it were, had used up too many of our economic chips and the impact on our economy was all the more severe.

Before, however, we move on to consider the employment crisis which has developed since 1980 I should like to comment further on the nature of some aspects of our economic and social development in the 1970s. First, regarding external migration, an important factor was that many of the young people who entered the labour market in large numbers during the early part of this decade had rather different attitudes from their predecessors. They were better educated and had grown up in a more liberal environment. They did not necessarily accept emigration as an automatic escape route and believed that their own country should be able to provide them with an adequate way of life. An entirely new feature, however, was not so much that fewer young people left the country, but that large numbers of former emigrants returned — a phenomenon which continued unabated throughout the decade, even during the recession of 1974-76. Previous experience would have suggested that, on the contrary, such depressed circumstances would have sparked off greater emigration. However it must be remembered that the economic downturn of this period was world-wide and conditions in Britain (the traditional destination for many of our emigrants) were no better than they were here. In earlier periods, irrespective of the economic circumstances, the British labour market would have had greater attractions to offer not only in the way of jobs but because of its generally better welfare and social insurance provisions. However by the mid-1970s Irish welfare benefits had been brought to a state of near quality *vis-a-vis* those of our larger neighbour, a process put in train at the time of our entry into the EEC.

The *employment* expansion which took place in the 1970s was quite different from that achieved in the preceding decade. It is true that job creation in manufacturing industry and building again contributed to the gains made, but these were now on a smaller scale. The labour market during this time, in Ireland as in other western countries, was characterised by a huge increase in employment in services. Much of this was in non-commercial public sector activities such as the civil service and in the education and health areas. The various magnitudes involved are perhaps best illustrated as follows; throughout the 1970s for every ten additional jobs outside of agriculture, no less than five were in public sector services, two were in manufacturing and building, while private service activities such as wholesaling and retailing, finance and banking and various forms of personal service contributed a further three jobs.

Obviously the expansion in public service employment had to be sustained from taxation sources. As the decade progressed this put an increasing strain on the national resources, a factor which was accentuated by the economic downturns. A further troubling sign was that the increases achieved in private services were rather narrowly based and tended to be heavily concentrated in certain economic sub-sectors such as banking, finance and insurance which, despite its relatively small size, contributed very significantly to the overall level of job creation. Thus as the end of the 1970s approached, even though on the face of it, much had been achieved in the way of employment creation, the foundations on which the more recent gains were based were fragile. It was inevitable that once the economy again encountered heavy weather, the consequences could be serious.

The economic deterioration which we have suffered since the renewed onset of recession at the beginning of 1980 has been very substantial. The longstanding decline in the numbers at work in agriculture has continued but in addition there has been a tremendous employment shake-out in the manufacturing and building sectors; a halt has been brought to expansion in the numbers at work in the public sector because of budgetary constraints; some significant employment gains have again been recorded in the private services area but these have not come anywhere near matching the reduction in other sectors. Thus the overall level of employment throughout the entire economy has fallen — by nearly 50,000 since 1980. The total numbers available for work have, however, continued to grow with the result that unemployment has now reached quite unprecedented heights; it currently stands at about 225,000 and, even allowing for some recent improvement, it could begin to approach a quarter of a million by early 1986. Emigration has re-emerged even if, as yet, on what appears to be a modest scale.

One may well ask why the degree of social discontent has not been more severe given that much lower unemployment levels sparked off protests in the 1950s. Part of the reason relates to the higher unemployment benefits now paid, which mitigate the financial ill-effects of unemployment, particularly in the early stages after job loss. Another factor may be involvement in the growing black economy, even though the extent of this is difficult to gauge.

There are certain special features of the current economic crisis which need to be emphasised. It is true that part of the underlying reason is what we call 'cyclical' in economic terms — in other words it was precipitated by one of the periodic down-turns in the level of economic activity which have characterised world trade for a very long time. However, it is now clear that other more fundamental changes have been taking place in the overall structure of employment — arising from the rundown of traditional industries, the introduction of new technology, changing work practices and other such reasons. As a result new problems are emerging — for example sizeable numbers of redundant workers who present serious difficulties of re-integration into employment. The use of new technologies also raises the possibility of being able to generate greater output but with the direct involvement of fewer workers — not only in new manufacturing processes but also in some service areas (for example in administration and office work arising from the use of computerised methods). When this scenario is set alongside the prospect of continuing growth in the numbers available for work, the implications for future unemployment levels are obvious.

This worrying perspective has not unexpectedly given rise to quite an intense debate as to how we might address these problems. Some take the view that the market economy as we know it is capable of providing the required levels of job creation but that the labour market must respond to the new environment by becoming more flexible. In other words, the potential for generating the required number of jobs is there, but the market is inhibited from achieving these goals as it creaks and groans beneath the weight of interventionist legislation relating to social security, discrimination, unfair dismissals, minimum wages and so on. Proponents of this view support their arguments by pointing to the recent employment experience in other countries. Over the ten years to 1983, almost 18 million extra jobs were created in North America, 5 million in Japan, compared with a net loss of 1½ million in Europe. Others however view this approach as a charter for renewed exploitation and see progress in employment creation being achieved, not so much by deregulation, but by a concentration on education and training to meet the needs of new technology which should in turn lead to a more flexible and mobile workforce; if despite all such initiatives, unemployment remains unacceptably high then the state should intervene, either by expanding employment in the public sector in the conventional sense, or by other means such as special work creation schemes. Proponents of the latter view point to the example of the Scandinavian countries, particularly Sweden, which have combined effective regulation of the labour market with a good employment record and relatively low levels of unemployment.

Each approach has its merits and disadvantages. While the introduction of more flexibility into the labour market may lead to a measure of employment creation (but hardly on a sufficient scale to make a dent in the current levels of unemployment) it is also likely, if carried too far, to create what is called greater 'segmentation' in the labour market. There would be, on the one hand, a core group of operatives in more permanent higher forms of work (and I would include many employers in this context) within whose power would lie the reallocation and redeployment of human and other resources within enterprises and across the economy as a whole. On the other hand, the greater freedom given to employers to hire and fire, adjust wages and determine work practices is likely to lead to the emergence of a large mobile group of workers, who may move with relative ease from one job to another but who would find it difficult to attain stable employment. For the individual such a situation of job insecurity would be very difficult to break out of, since the tenuous nature of the jobs held would virtually preclude the acquisition of proper training or more advanced forms of work experience. Thus while deregulation may initially lead to efficiency gains and employment expansion in individual firms in the short term, the

longer-term prospects for the economy as a whole could be damaged by a deterioration in the level of skill and competence in the
workforce as a whole.

Greater involvement by the state in job creation activities also has
its disadvantages. It must be remembered that jobs created directly
by the state have to be funded from taxation sources. The manner
in which these funds are obtained can have a disadvantageous effect
on employment in the private sector, which may offset the benefits
of any new public sector jobs. Public sector organisations can
develop an unwarranted momentum of their own and become too
large, cumbersome and inefficient. While new ventures can be fairly
readily initiated, it can be extremely difficult, because of political
and other pressures to terminate or even scale down activities which
have clearly outlived their usefulness. In this sense the public sector
lacks the flexibility and undoubted vitality which characterises private enterprise. If an expansion in public sector numbers were to be
accompanied by sizeable increases in the earnings of public
employees, the whole approach would be unsustainable, indeed
unthinkable in the context of our present financial position.

However public sector involvement in job creation has begun to
take new and different forms. Currently across many countries in
the western hemisphere new avenues are being explored to aid
employment creation, particularly measures aimed at activating
local labour markets and especially joint programmes involving
community groups and state agencies. Many of these activities fall
within what has become known as 'Third Sector' (after the state and
private enterprise) and the concept has been taken quite some distance in a number of countries, in Belgium for example. So far however this general movement has tended to give rise to many and varied activities which cannot, as yet, be seen as a cohesive influence in
promoting job creation on a substantial scale.

Another school of thought suggests that the solution of the
unemployment problem in Ireland lies in accepting or even
encouraging emigration. If one views the problem essentially in
terms of numbers, emigration has acted as an economic and social
safety valve in the past. Why, therefore, cannot this situation be
realised again, thus reducing the scale of our domestic problems to
more manageable proportions? Others view the possibility of
increased emigration within a broader community or European
dimension. Young Irish people are now better educated and many

have studied at least one continental language; they have full mobility and employment rights across all EEC member states. It is not unreasonable therefore to expect them to avail of the opportunities in other more economically advanced centres.

Many find the concept of emigration envisaged in the latter pan-European context acceptable — particularly if it were to involve the acquisition of skills and experience which could be of ultimate benefit to this country if the young emigrants subsequently returned (as many in the past have done). This approach may indeed gain greater acceptance over the coming years as the youth population in all of the larger European countries begin to fall, thus opening up the possibility of better employment opportunities in youth labour markets abroad.

However the positive encouragement of emigration as a means of solving our problems, divorced from any other considerations, is another matter altogether. Those who are inclined to espouse this approach should reflect on the possible consequences. In the first place it is tantamount to an open admission of defeat and if governments were to adopt this stance it could create a very dangerous degree of despondency in the community as a whole. Our experience with emigration in the past is surely not so remote for us to be unaware of the possible consequences for a society which allows, or encourages, its more vigorous and creative members to drift away in large numbers. I can well recall the sense of despondency and near despair in the 1950s in a society which was inward looking, ultra conservative in attitude, and lacking in self-confidence and creativity. The policy of promoting emigration could have serious long-term consequences as it would eliminate part of the very human resource base on which our future development would depend.

Let me conclude by saying that I see merit in different aspects of the various labour market approaches which I have described. Perhaps the path which offers the best hope of alleviating the unemployment problem is one which involves keeping an open mind and drawing on the best which each approach has to offer. To my mind proposed solutions to the problem are now all too often linked to different forms of ideology.

With regard to the deregulation argument there *are* advantages to be gained from having greater labour market flexibility, even if this process is not pursued to the extent of removing the necessary safeguards which have been introduced to protect the weaker members of our society. I would mention, for example, the elimination of restrictive practices and obstacles to the introduction of new technologies and work methods. Greater flexibility in the labour market would also help to check the growth of the black economy which is now a sizeable element in society as a whole.

Nor can one indefinitely rule out the involvement of the public sector in the job creation process. The problems which we face are now of such a magnitude that we cannot ignore the vast potential of the state in the battle against unemployment. It is true that we have had some recent unfortunate experiences with public enterprises, but this should not be allowed to impede the search for new and more appropriate means of exploiting this resource.

A further aspect of importance is to bring the question of employment promotion more to the forefront in the formulation of general economic and social policy. All to frequently in the past the disadvantageous consequences for employment of new measures in the taxation, social security and other areas have not been adequately recognised.

The attainment of progress in tackling the current employment crisis will not be easy. If we are to make headway within the context of the political and economic structures as we now know them, all interests involved will have to demonstrate more flexibility and be prepared to concede on some issues long held to be sacred. Currently the Irish government is preparing a new manpower strategy designed to cover the period up to the early 1990s. I would hope that this might provide an appropriate framework within which some of the above-mentioned concepts and ideas might be accommodated.

4. Industry: The Revolution Unfinished

Kieran A. Kennedy

Manufacturing production in Ireland is now four times higher than in 1960, and has replaced agriculture as the dominant source of exports. This is quite a revolution. But in some ways the revolution is far from complete. The industrial revolution in other countries brought about a large rise in manufacturing employment. This did not happen in Ireland, even though employment creation was the chief goal of industrial policy. The share of manufacturing in total employment in 1985, at less than one-fifth, is only a little higher than it was twenty-five years ago, and is far lower than in most industrial countries at the same stage in their development. Ireland has few large manufacturing enterprises, even allowing for its small size. Many of its older firms have closed down or contracted, and there has been heavy dependence on new foreign enterprise, foreign technology and foreign marketing to fill the void. This pattern of development gave rise to weaknesses, which were cruelly exposed in the difficult economic conditions of recent years — so much so that we must now make a fresh start in our approach to industrialisation. How did all this come about?

THE TRANSITION IN THE 1950s

The 1950s marked an important transition in Irish industrial development. The strategy laid down then was to hold sway for the next quarter-century — though it was of course refined and extended over time. In the 1950s, Irish manufacturing industry consisted chiefly of firms producing for a home market protected by extensive tariffs and quotas. Most of the firms dated from the 1930s when the first major effort was made to industrialise. Despite the attempt to keep Irish production in Irish hands, there was a sizeable minority of foreign establishments — mainly British subsidiaries — which had been set up following protection to preserve sales in Ireland. The small size of the Irish market precluded most firms — native or foreign — from reaching an efficient scale, and little or no effort had been made to prepare them for entry into export markets. Indeed many of the firms did no more than assemble imported components.

The limitations of such an introverted manufacturing sector became widely recognised in the 1950s, a time when the whole of the western world was moving to dismantle protectionist barriers and restore free trade. From early in that decade Irish policy shifted progressively to an outgoing direction. Grants were introduced to cover part of the cost of investment in new manufacturing enterprises, particularly those geared to the export market. Profits from manufactured exports were freed from taxation. Efforts were begun to attract foreign enterprise. The Public Capital Programme launched by the inter-party government in the late 1940s had also done much to provide roads, electricity, housing and other facilities needed for industry. By the time that T.K. Whitaker's classic work, *Economic Development,* welded these measures into a coherent framework, the foundations of the new industrial policy were already in place, though the dismantling of the old had not yet started.

THE MOVE TO FREE TRADE 1960-1973
The export-oriented approach initiated in the early 1950s took time to make an impact. The new agencies had to feel their way in uncharted terrain. Also the home market was depressed, due to the poor marketing conditions for agricultural exports, and the harsh budgets in the early and middle years of the decade. But from the late 1950s onwards there was a sustained improvement. Between 1960 and 1973 the volume of manufacturing output more than doubled. Employment, however, grew much more slowly — by about one-third over this period. This was because the amount of capital per worker increased greatly, because efficiency in production rose all round, and because the new activities used much less labour per unit of output than the older activities.

Industries which expanded rapidly at this time included chemicals, mineral products, metals and electrical equipment. Food manufacturers also increased in volume though not much in sophistication. The other traditional industries, most of which grew up under protection — such as clothing, footwear, leather, furniture and printing — lagged behind but were still important for employment. Apart from brief intervals, the growth of manufactured exports stayed at a high rate. While manufactured imports also grew rapidly, nevertheless the economy moved steadily from being almost a total net importer towards balance in trade in manufactures.

The benefits of this progress were felt throughout the economy. With exports now expanding rapidly, the government could safely encourage the growth of home demand, especially through building activity. This in turn fed back to manufacturing firms catering for the home market, which induced further growth in electricity, transport and communications. It began to look as if the industrial boom had put the economy on a path where every step forward made the next one easier.

In the flowering climate of optimism and self-confidence, attention focused on dismantling protection and completing the move to free trade. This led in the early 1960s to unilateral tariff cuts and the ending of restrictions on foreign enterprise; to the free-trade agreement with Britain in 1965; and to joining the European Community in 1973. These events have been examined already in the first two essays and there is no need to go into the details here. But it is worth noting that the changes were not mere *economic* adjustments. The ease with which they took place could readily divert attention from the profound *political* transformation.[1] This involved the major political party, Fianna Fáil, in reversing the policy of economic nationalism which had first brought it to power in 1932 and which sustained it in government for much of the next generation. During that period strong vested interests had formed in the protected industries to maintain the status quo. In bringing about the changes with so little social friction, tribute must be paid to the pragmatic skills of Seán Lemass, to the enlightened support given by the other political parties, and to the constructive rôle of the business and trade union leaders.

Great imagination and creativity were also shown by the public administration in pushing forward the industrial drive, and a degree of co-operation with the other social partners was achieved which had no precedents in Irish history. Detailed surveys of the strengths and weaknesses of Irish industry were carried out in the early 1960s with commendable speed, and led to a scheme of adaptation grants to re-equip the older industries for free trade. There were some teething troubles in the development agencies, and for a number of years responsibility was shared between two main bodies: the Industrial Development Authority (IDA), which was responsible for seeking new proposals, and An Fóras Tionscail, which funded them. Eventually in 1969, both functions were assigned to the IDA. Under the dynamic leadership of Michael Killeen, the IDA went on to command world-wide admiration for its skill in attracting foreign industry — so much so that its methods have been widely copied by promotional bodies abroad.

THE OIL CRISES AND DEPRESSIONS

In the early 1970s, there were great hopes that entry to the EEC would give a new impetus to industry. Ireland by then had a track record in drawing foreign enterprises; these enterprises had fared well and were highly profitable; there was a plentiful supply of labour, then scarce in Europe; and this labour had shown itself capable of adapting well to the needs of industry. Now with the prospect of free access to a market of 250 million persons, the sky seemed the limit. The IDA spoke confidently of generating 10,000 extra jobs a year in manufacturing which, together with the employment induced in other sectors, would make full employment at last a realistic aim.

This rosy prospect was embraced so eagerly that the thorns were scarcely seen. But the thorns were there none the less. Much of the increase in output and exports had come from new foreign industry, and little of the older protected part had responded to the new incentives. They were still heavily reliant on the home market. Their vulnerability in the face of free trade did not show up for some time after the signing of the Anglo-Irish Free Trade Area Agreement, which was phased over a number of years. The first tariff reductions, because they started from such a high level, caused little pain; but with each succeeding cut the squeeze on profits tightened. By the early 1970s job losses were becoming significant, and the now all too familiar word 'redundancy' first entered into every day speech. Job losses in the older firms were likely to accelerate in the face of the even greater competition in the home market after EEC entry.

But even the expected gains from new industry were thwarted at first by the oil crisis towards the end of 1973 and the resulting depression. The flow of foreign enterprise is always highly sensitive to the state of the world economy, and Ireland's continued industrial expansion had come to depend on that inflow. In the depression following the first oil shock, manufacturing output fell by one-tenth.

This depression was short-lived, however, and by the middle of 1976 production had recovered to the previous peak level. There was a buoyant stream of new projects, and output continued to expand rapidly until the end of 1979, when it was nearly two-fifths higher than in 1973. Employment was slower to pick up due to offsetting job losses in older industries, and it was not until 1979 that total employment in manufacturing recovered fully.

No sooner did it seem that Ireland was at last about to realise the promised benefits of the EEC connection, than the second large rise in oil prices occurred towards the end of 1979. The world depression following this shock was much more prolonged. Manufacturing production stagnated for three whole years (1980, 1981 and 1982). As in the previous world depression, the inflow of new foreign projects slackened. More ominous still, the new foreign industries set up some years earlier were losing jobs nearly as fast as the traditional sectors.

Since 1983, there has been a recovery in manufacturing output, which was nearly one-third higher in 1985 than in 1980. Employment, however, has continued to fall — to well below the level at the time we joined the Common Market. The reason is that recovery has been concentrated in a few 'sunrise' industries — notably electronics and pharmaceuticals — that have very low employment in relation to their total sales. These industries seem to be highly profitable, though part of the profits may be due to artificial pricing in order to maximise tax reliefs, and part may be needed to pay for research and marketing at the firms' headquarters. At all events, a worrying new feature is that a large portion of the profit or surplus earned by foreign enterprise in Ireland is being taken out of the country — to the tune of £940 million in 1984. This is part of the infamous 'black hole' in the Irish balance of payments and, together with interest payments on government borrowing abroad, it constitutes a huge draw on export earnings.

So much for the recent experience of new foreign enterprise. The situation of the traditional sector is even worse. Employment in many of the larger firms has been either wiped out entirely or greatly reduced. Among the big names of Irish industry, Fords and Dunlops have vanished altogether, while employment in Guinness' brewery is being cut to one-third of what it was twenty-five years ago. True, there has been the odd success story — like Smurfits, now a multinational in its own right, and Cement-Roadstone, becoming one. But on the whole, the belief that competition would whip native industries into shape has not been sustained. Instead it snuffed them out.

Indeed the position in regard to native industry would be much bleaker were it not for the small firms. The IDA Small Industry Programme begun in 1967 has evoked a heartening response and has helped to create and expand a wide range of small industries. As in many other countries over the past decade, Ireland has found that small firms are a better bet for extra employment than large. The bulk of employment, however, is still in large firms and when these are shedding so many jobs, the small firms cannot fully make up the difference. Moveover, an industrial structure in which all the firms were small would not be very satisfactory. Small firms find it hard to export, and must often rely on the big firms to provide a market. A large scale of operation is often needed also to develop new technology. So far, few of the Irish small firms have shown the potential to reach such a scale.[2]

RE-ORIENTATION OF INDUSTRIAL STRATEGY

Given the upheaval in the world economy over the past decade, no industrial policy could have saved us from a slowing down in industrial performance compared with the 1960s. We also added to the difficulties ourselves by continuing to press for higher pay and more government hand-outs. Yet it would be wrong to suggest that there were no flaws in the industrial policy itself. Well before the decline was clearly visible, some critics had begun to sound the alarm bells. The palm for the most penetrating of the early critiques must undoubtedly go to Charles Cooper and Noel Whelan for a study completed in February 1972 and published early in the following year by the National Science Council.[3] They not only diagnosed the main weaknesses in the evolving structure of industry, but they also threw light on the root causes of those weaknesses. And they went on to sketch the outlines of an alternative strategy, which corresponded in all essentials to what was to be advocated a decade later, at much greater expense, following a major review of industrial policy.

Cooper and Whelan began with the paradox that while Irish industry was becoming a significant exporter of science-based products, yet this production did not draw on Irish science and technology. They found the explanation of this paradox in the structure of industry. The new foreign plants, which were chiefly responsible for the exports, drew their technology from their parent firms and made little use of Irish research and development (R & D). By the same token, these plants relied heavily also on their overseas affiliates to provide the market for their products. The plants were little more than production platforms which were located in Ireland to take advantage of the generous industrial grants and tax concessions, political stability, access to markets, and the availability of labour at rates of pay still well below the industrialised nations. While in no sense fly-by-night operations, still they had few linkages with the rest of the economy. The older section of Irish manufacturing did not make much use of domestic R & D either. Protection had left a legacy of undersized firms, involved mainly in the final assembly of products for sale on the small home market. These firms had neither the incentive nor the resources to engage in innovative R & D or marketing. Cooper and Whelan argued that the prevailing policy would not correct these deficiencies: on the contrary, it would reinforce them. In particular the policy did not face up to the task of building a selection of strong Irish companies geared to world markets.

Now that our sights were set on world markets, why should it matter then whether the firms were foreign or indigenous? Cooper and Whelan did not base their approach on narrow nationalist grounds, and they were not against the selective use of foreign enterprise. But for two reasons above all they held that the social benefits of foreign enterprise were overstated. First, they foresaw that, though repatriation of profits were not then a problem, it could become so one day; and they argued that the propensity to transfer profits abroad would be less in the case of Irish firms. Second, the use of foreign technology and marketing was a poor substitute for developing these talents at home. Ireland was exporting expensively-trained scientists, engineers and technicians, and Cooper and Whelan believed that strong native firms would use this resource to build an enduring innovative capacity of their own.

Other critics elaborated and documented the shortcomings noted by Cooper and Whelan.[4] But while such criticisms were not entirely ignored, they were shrugged off as long as progress seemed to be satisfactory.[5] By the late 1970s, however, it was officially accepted that a thorough independent review of industrial policy was called for, and the National Economic and Social Council was asked to undertake it. This review resulted in several valuable reports,[6] the most widely publicised being known as the Telesis Report, called after the American consultancy group which prepared it. While the Telesis Report praised Irish industrial policy and the good work of the agencies implementing it, the report also endorsed many of the earlier criticisms. In particular it concluded that the goals of the policy had not been achieved.

The Telesis Report recommended a modified strategy similar to that proposed by Cooper and Whelan ten years earlier. The approach should be more selective, giving priority to building a limited number of large Irish companies to serve markets not only here and in Britain but in the whole Common Market and beyond. The key to the success of these companies would lie in high-quality marketing, innovation and the development of native skills. The companies eventually should be capable of standing on their own and performing such functions themselves, rather than relying indefinitely on the state. The Report had no objection to foreign enterprise, provided it strengthened the long-term potential of industry in Ireland. But the Report stressed most of all the need to foster native industry, since in its view 'no country has succeeded in developing high levels of industrial income without developing a strong indigenous sector'.

It must be said that the critics have all been better at showing where we wanted to arrive than how we were to get there, and at what cost. As it is, the strategy is not cheap: in 1982, for example, the amount of government spending (including tax reliefs) on industry has been estimated at £750 million,[7] which compares with total manufacturing value added in that year of £2,300 million. But the Telesis Report acknowledged that 'creating and sustaining jobs in indigenous firms is far more difficult and expensive than doing so in foreign-owned firms' (p. 232). It is probable, then, that had a Telesis-type strategy been in operation earlier, industrial expansion over the past 25 years would have been slower and more costly. On the other hand, the approach, if successful, would have laid a firmer basis for long-term advance.

Great problems beset the government now in re-shaping the long-term industrial strategy in the face of enormous short-term pressures. When the world economic outlook is so uncertain, the risks to be taken are far greater. When the immediate need for jobs is desperate, it is not easy to turn away any employment opportunities even if they are not ideal from a long-term viewpoint. When resources are scarce, it is hard to contemplate still greater funding for industry, although this could be necessary to develop the native firms. Indeed, it may even seem paradoxical to switch the emphasis of policy to the indigenous sector only after so much of it has already gone to the wall. Yet, a new factor has emerged which strengthens the case for such a re-orientation. Not only has the volume of foreign enterprise been depleted by the uncertain outlook for the world economy, but more countries are competing for the reduced volume. The richest nations of Europe are now giving incentives to foreign firms that in some cases match or even exceed those offered by Ireland.

These difficulties may explain, if not excuse, the evident indecision in government about industrial policy. More than two years elapsed after the publication of the Telesis Report before a White Paper on the subject was published in July 1984. Although the White Paper endorses the Telesis strategy in principle, its practical proposals seem to fall far short of what Telesis had in mind. As well, it has taken nearly three years for the proposed National Development Corporation, promised in the *Programme of Government* in 1982, to reach the legislative stage. There are plausible arguments both for and against this proposal, but no good argument for agonising so long about it. Ireland has also lagged far behind other countries in developing exports of health and educational services, which may often be more suited than manufacturing to the aptitudes and aspirations of the Irish labour force. Much remains to be done in the marketing, processing and farming of agricultural products if we are to realise our potential in the export of foods. The management of forestry is still in the hands of the civil service even though countless experts have advised that the job could be done better by a commercial state body.

CONCLUSION

Looking at the industrialisation of Ireland over the past twenty-five years, the overall picture is one of much progress marred by underlying flaws. We staked our money on the hare of foreign enterprise rather than on the tortoise of native industry. The hare ran well for a time and impressive gains in output were achieved, with even more impressive gains in exports. Until the upheaval in the world economy following the oil crises, industry set the pace for a rapid improvement in living standards.

Yet the race is not always to the swiftest. The approach produced quick but not lasting results. Near the end of our period, the Telesis Report characterised Ireland as a country with few high-skilled, high-technology enterprises; where indigenous exports were small and confined to a limited range of markets; where Irish firms were not able to meet the sub-supply needs of foreign firms; where small firms existed chiefly in low-skilled activities in which competition from abroad was absent; where there was little co-operation between primary producers and processors of native raw materials; and where foreign-owned industry showed inadequate promise for substantial improvement. In fact, it would be hard to dispute the considered verdict of Dermot McAleese that 'in respect of the key objective of industrial policy (i.e., employment), the business sector has been found wanting'.[8]

In brief, the industrial programme failed to dynamise the largest section of manufacturing — the domestic industries. It did not go far enough in developing native skills in technology and marketing, the key elements of self-sustaining growth. The foundations of the industrial superstructure therefore lacked depth. Until this depth is secured, the Irish industrial revolution must be judged unfinished.

5. Agriculture and Other Natural Resources

Robert O'Connor

Twenty-five years ago Ireland was not thought of as a country rich in natural resources. Nevertheless it had a low density of population in relation to the agricultural land area; as an island its marine resources were potentially large and almost completely unexploited; and though we did not value it much then, Ireland had an almost completely unspoiled environment. Moveover significant mineral and gas deposits were subsequently found and there are prospects of further discoveries.

How successful have we been in exploiting the considerable natural resource potential available; to what extent and why have we failed to use it to the best advantage and in what ways have we damaged the natural environment?

The short answer to these questions is that even though there have been remarkable developments in technology over the years we have not exploited all our natural resources as well as we should. In 1960 about one-third of the national income was generated in the natural resource sectors, agriculture, forestry, fishing, mining, food processing and beverages. Today the proportion has been halved; only about one-sixth of our income comes from these sources. The trend has been similar in the overall numbers employed though in some sectors there have been slight increases in numbers.

These figures, however, are not as bad as they might appear. Agriculture for instance which is a large sector in Ireland has declined relative to industry and the services in all the developed countries so that what is happening here is not at all unusual. Actually there has been considerable growth in the volume output of agriculture and some of the other sectors over the past 25 years.

A number of developments have shaped our economic destiny in recent years but those which have had the greatest effect on the natural resources environment were accession to the EEC in 1973 and the two severe oil shocks in the 1970s. The discovery of valuable mineral deposits in Tynagh, Co. Galway in 1961 was another important development. This led to a spate of explorations in Ireland and to comparable successes at other sites.

EEC ACCESSION

EEC accession in 1973 must be regarded as the most important event in Irish history since Independence. It affected the whole economy in various ways but in the natural resource area it had its more profound effect on agriculture and fisheries and to a lesser extent on forestry.

Agriculture: In the early years of the 1960s Irish agriculture was in a very depressed state. Farm incomes were low and there had been little growth since the Second World War. Trade was virtually confined to the low priced United Kingdom market and that market did not provide a very remunerative outlet for our produce. In the circumstances the government was forced to extend economic aid to farmers on a massive scale, throughout the 1960s. The result was that by 1972 state expenditure in relation to agriculture accounted for one-third of farmers' incomes and was taking up one-sixth of total tax revenue.

With this background it is not surprising that EEC membership was warmly welcomed not alone by farmers but by the great majority of the population who in 1972 voted by a four to one majority in favour of EEC entry. We were entering a high priced market with guaranteed prices for most farm products. Capital grants for farm improvements were available and there were various subventions from Brussels for underdeveloped areas and infrastructure. Prosperity was around the corner.

In the event EEC membership proved to be more turbulent than anticiapted. Prices had risen in the early 1970s in anticipation of EEC entry but there was a sharp fall in 1974 as a result of a crisis in the world cattle industry. Prices recovered quickly again up to 1978 when it appeared that the earlier expectations were justified. The good times had come and it looked like they were here to stay. In 1979 however the tide turned. Agricultural prices in that year rose much less than the rate of inflation and farm incomes dropped substantially. The 1979 depression was followed by a more severe decline in 1980; and over the two years 1979 and 1980 average income per farmer was almost halved, wiping out all the gains since 1973.

Even in retrospect it is difficult to appreciate the havoc which this set-back brought on an economy highly dependent on agriculture. In 1978 farmers were on top of the world, building new houses, buying machinery, borrowing for investment, spending freely in the local towns and generating large-scale employment in the service sector. Two years later they were on their knees and had taken with them all those depending on their spending. There were casualties everywhere. The feed, fertiliser and machinery industries became decimated. Local shops and garages were in hock, and farm house building had ceased. It was like the aftermath of a battle with casualties all around and the government frantically seeking EEC aid to salvage as much as possible.

To try and apportion blame for what happened is futile. The large price increases between 1974 and 1978 fuelled unrealistic expectations, the lending institutions fanned the flame further by making imprudent advances, for land purchase, but the root cause was inflation of input and living cost prices which could not be matched on the output side. Wise men will say that this experience has taught us a lesson which will never be forgotten but that is wishful thinking. There are some things we never learn and one of these is the control of unrealistic expectations. We oscillate continuously from optimism to pessimism in response to peer group pressure. The 'band-wagon' effect is endemic.

After 1980 matters improved somewhat but even in 1983 real income per worker in agriculture had not returned to its 1973 level despite a fall of 25% in the farm labour force over the period. The agricultural boom was over and with food surpluses piling up all over Europe there is now little prospect of a return to the heady 1978 position. Milk output is being restricted by quotas; beef is under pressure. There is a strong drive to lower grain prices and through this route all meat prices. The only consolation is that Irish farmers could be even worse off outside the EEC. Dependency on world markets without large export aids would mean bankruptcy for many.

Though Irish farmers fared well in terms of income in the period 1970 to 1978 this was due more to high prices than to increased production. Various studies have shown that our land is not being used to anything like its full potential. The expansion that has occurred has been confined to about two-thirds of the land area of the state. The remaining third, which is operated by older people, is showing practically no growth in output.

Another area of disappointment is in food processing. Though we export about 60% of output a very high proportion goes out in an unprocessed or slightly processed form thus giving low off-farm employment. Efficiency in Irish agricultue has improved, but some people are asking what kind of efficiency is it that sheds labour to add to the dole queues while unprocessed food piles up in intervention stores. We have taken the easy way of selling traditional products at low guaranteed prices rather than developing new products for higher priced markets. This is a dangerous situation in view of the pressure on the EEC budget; it leaves agriculture unduly dependent on artificial outlets and without contact with real markets, while it reduces jobs in food processing, one of the few industries where work could be created.

Further areas of concern are in the production and marketing of vegetables. High imports over the past few years are due mainly to poor quality and bad presentation, matters which require urgent attention. There is a danger also to our long established bacon trade through over-salting and poor quality generally. Nor have we reacted to the modern drive for leaner meat. Our beef and lamb exports are over-fat for continental markets and are suffering large price discounts. But we are gradually beginning to learn. The competition on the food market at home, and abroad, is hurting where it matters most, in producer's and processors' pockets. This is a powerful incentive for change.

Fishing: At the time of joining the EEC strong fears were expressed concerning the fate of the fishing industry. Considerable development had taken place in the previous decade but it was now feared that this expansion would be halted as a result of the proposed Common Fisheries Policy which aimed at allowing all member states to fish anywhere within community waters. In these circumstances the Irish small boat fleet could be decimated by the large British and continental trawlers.

These fears were well-grounded at the time. There was bitter experience of large foreign boats sweeping around our shores and sucking up every type of aquatic animal that moved. Since then, as a result of hard bargaining, the so-called 'beach to beach' policy has been deferred, probably indefinitely. Member states are allowed exclusive fishing rights within six to twelve mile zones of their coasts thus giving the small boat owners a chance of survival. Also, Ireland has been treated fairly generously in regard to EEC quotas and as a result our catch has more than doubled since 1975. It has gone up ten times since 1960 from 20,000 to 200,000 tonnes.

There have of course been many difficulties along the way. The increased landings are due to the expansion of the large boat fleet which has enabled crews to fish safely in distant waters. These boats are however very expensive. Though subsidised heavily by Bórd Iascaigh Mhara (BIM), the annual repayments by a skipper could be as much at £250,000 per annum. He would need to catch a lot of fish to meet this and all other costs.

Another difficulty relates to the supply of fish. The adoption of 200 mile limits by third countries has pushed many EEC boats out of traditional grounds and into waters off the Irish coast. As a result these waters have become over-fished and the catching of herring has had to be suspended in some areas. The current economic depression and the high price of oil has not helped matters either. The result is that many boat owners are now in financial difficulty and over the past few years a substantial number of boats subvented by BIM were repossessed.

However, taken all in all progress in fleet development and catching have been impressive but the same cannot be said for the marketing of fish and fish products. A high proportion of the catch is sold in bulk form at low prices. Only a small proportion is processed into products which would give high onshore employment. The aim must be to increase the processing sector substantially and expand research so as to identify new products which can be sold profitably on home and foreign markets. Landings must also be expanded further so as to improve continuity of supply. Towards this end BIM has introduced an exploratory fishing programme to identify new grounds hitherto unfished, and locate commercial species not covered by EEC quotas. It is hoped that this enterprise will prove successful.

There is scope also for the development of aquaculture (the artificial rearing of fish). Trout and shellfish farming are showing good profits. In 1984 we produced 400 tonnes of farmed salmon and it is expected that more than double this amount will be produced within the next few years. If this happens, as is now quite likely, the weight of farmland salmon will be greater than our total wild catch which is declining gradually as a result of almost uncurtailed drift net fishing for salmon on the high seas. To date politicians of all parties have shied away from the drift netting problem and it seems now that they are prepared to preside over the demise of our most prized fish. It will be a sad day when this happens.

Forestry: Ireland's mild climate and relatively fertile soils provide an environment very suitable for tree growth. Yet forests cover only about 6% of the land area of the state which is the least wooded country in Europe. There are several million acres of wet marshy land in the country highly suited to tree growing which are almost non-productive in agriculture.

Since the foundation of the state, most of the planning is carried on by the Department of Forestry, and state forests now account for 80% of the wooded area. In other European countries, more than half the forest area is owned by the private sector, mainly by small holders. In France, 3 million farmers have small forests on their farms. This contrasts greatly with our situation where few small farmers have any trees at all and where organised resistance to private planting has occurred in some areas; companies who have purchased land for forestry have in some cases been faced with strong local opposition.

In recent years the imbalance in our forest ownership as between the public and private sector is causing considerable unease both at government and EEC levels. It is recognised that the Forestry Department can grow trees very well but its ability to market timber is limited. The tender system which it uses is considered by the trade to be too inflexible and would need to be supplemented by a strong private sector involvement.

In order to increase private plantings the EEC Western Package includes a good private forestry element. Indeed it contains the most generous grant aid available for any scheme within the communtiy and, if availed of, ensures that small private tree stands could be established at almost no cost to the grower.

There is, of course, one major problem associated with private forestry. Because of the length of time it takes a forest to mature the first returns do not come until after fifteen years and the final return takes forty years to realise. Tree growing, therefore, regardless of its financial return, is not very attractive to older people. To get over this problem the Irish Co-Operative Organisation Society is trying to organise through the EEC a scheme to give returns at an earlier date. Under this scheme a farmer planting a crop of trees would have the opportunity of forward selling the timber at a price related to the productivity of the land on which the timber is grown. He would thus receive an annual income each year on land which is currently yielding next to nothing in agriculture. If this scheme can be finalised it should have an important social, as well as an economic impact on the communities involved while at the same time increasing substantially the forest area of the country.

THE OIL CRISIS
During the period of cheap oil up to 1973 little official interest was taken in energy and only a small number of people were employed in the Power Section of the Department of Transport and Power. After the first oil shock in 1973 the Department was greatly expanded and in 1980 following the second shock in 1979 a separate Energy Department was formed. This Department is also responsible for mineral exploration. Prior to 1974 less than 20% of our total energy supply was home produced. At the present time native fuel makes up almost 40% of our primary energy requirements. The two main home produced fuels are peat and natural gas. Home produced coal and hydro-electric power supply only about 3% of our requirements.

Peat: Ireland is the largest producer of peat in the western world and second only to Russia in the entire world. Bórd na Móna was established in 1946 to develop our peat resources and has now taken over about 200,000 acres of bog for development.

In 1960 the Board employed 5,000 people and produced 2½ million tonnes of peat of which about 60% was used for electricity production. At that time about one-third of our electricity was produced from peat. In 1983 Bórd na Móna produced over 6 million tonnes of peat of which almost half was used by the ESB to produce about 18% of its electricity. In addition to its peat production Bórd na Móna (as well as private industry) produces large amounts of moss peat for gardening purposes, most of which is exported. Nowadays the Board employs 6,000 workers with a total wage bill of

£60m. per annum.

What of the future? The few sod peat power stations now in operation will be closed down by 1990 but it is expected that the Board will continue producing sods for domestic use until at least the end of the century. By that time household requirements are expected to be supplied by private producers in bogs which would be uneconomic for Bórd na Móna's large machines. The milled peat power stations are expected to continue until the year 2000, and beyond, unless other fuel prices drop considerably.

Offshore Oil and Gas: The first active interest in Ireland as a possible area for petroleum exploration was in 1959 when a group of American companies were given exclusive rights to explore and develop petroleum deposits in the whole of the country. A considerable amount of exploration was carried out on the mainland in the 1960s but petroleum was not found in commercially workable quantities. In 1969 interest shifted from the mainland to the continental shelf and in August 1973 the Marathon Company announced the discovery of a commerical gas field in the area south of Kinsale Head estimated to contain reserves of high quality natural gas capable of sustaining a steady output for twenty-two years. This find coinciding as it did with the first oil shock was followed by intense drilling operations but no oil was found in commercial quantities until 1984 when a number of small wells were drilled off Ardmore Head, Co. Waterford. Though none of these is exploitable on its own there are distinct possibilities that they can be put together to form one economic field. It has been estimated that such a field would yield about 5% of our total tax revenue for twenty years. The Ardmore finds and the continuing high oil prices in Ireland have stimulated a spate of new explorations and the prospects for further finds are very encouraging particularly in the Porcupine Bank. Within the past year there has been a second gas find off Kinsale which will have an important influence on our energy policy.

These new oil and gas finds will change the whole energy scenario of the country, particularly the gas discoveries. Unlike oil, gas cannot be readily exported in large quantities and must be used locally. It will, therefore, come into direct competition with existing fuels, making life very difficult for the suppliers of these products, particularly for Bórd na Móna. The level of pricing the different fuels is going to have a profound effect on usage but the employment which

Bórd na Móna creates in the rural areas is also an important factor which cannot be discounted.

MINERAL EXPLORATION

Base Metals: Ireland has been a significant base metal producer at several stages in her history but from the turn of the century up to 1961 Irish metal mining had declined to the extent that prospects for its revival seemed slight. In 1961, however, a valuable lead, zinc, copper and silver deposit was discovered at Tynagh, Co. Galway, which rapidly led to a boom in exploration in Ireland and to comparable successes at Silvermines, and Gortdrum, Co. Tipperary in 1964 and more recently to the discovery of very large and rich deposits of lead and zinc in Navan, Co. Meath. In 1970 production of copper and pyrite was resumed at Avoca, Co. Wicklow. Unfortunately, mining has now ceased at all these sites except Navan. The deposits at Tynagh and in Tipperary have run out, and a drop in the price of copper has led to the closing of the Avoca mine. These mines provided valuable income and employment in their respective areas during the periods of their operation but they produced little in the way of down stream activities. The erection of a smelter was ruled out because of its capital intensive nature, high energy requirements and its low employment content. Hence even if further large metal deposits are discovered, smeltering in Ireland is not likely to be considered an economic proposition.

Other minerals: The extraction of industrial minerals other than base metals is a smaller activity in terms of direct mining employment, but the degree of subsequent processing is greater. These minerals include gypsum for plasterboard and cement production; barytes for 'drilling mud' in oil exploration, silica for glass making as well as brick clays, magnesite, limestone, lime and road metals. A massive baryte deposit at Ballymore near Silvermines in Co. Tipperary is one of the world's largest baryte mines. The current mining rate is 200,000 tonnes per annum which is 40% of world production. The industrial development of talc from large deposits on Inishbofin Island, Co. Galway and from similar deposits near Westport, Co. Mayo is under condiseration while a recently commissioned plant near Drogheda is producing magnesite from local limestone and sea water.

THE ENVIRQNMENT

Increased economic growth brings many benefits, such as relief of poverty, reduction of involuntary emigration and improvement of housing standards. On the other hand it usually results in increased waste loads and additional environmental pressures. But economic growth, through education, also gives large numbers of people both the opportuntiy and the ability to appreciate nature and natural processes with a resultant demand for pure air, clean water and an attractive countryside. Thus growth and technology have given man the ability to destroy the quality of the environment and at the same time the desire to preserve it. Let us consider briefly how Ireland has fared in this conflict, particularly in regard to the quality of its water and air which are the main barometers of environmental stress.

Water pollution: Up to the first half of the twentieth century Ireland escaped the worst ravages of water pollution that were apparent in the more developed countries. This was mainly due to the low level of industrial development and to the fact that the bulk of the population lived in rural areas. However, the increase in industrial and agricultural activities has led to the discharge of greater quantities of waste into our water system. These wastes have created a number of localised situations where serious damage has been caused. The available data show that eleven of the country's larger lakes are polluted to a considerable extent and in at least two of these, Loughs Ennell and Sheelin, there has been a significant loss of beneficial use. In addition, some 4,000 miles of rivers and streams are polluted, some of them very seriously. In general the condition of our coastal waters is satisfactory but in the urbanised reaches of some of these waters there is considerable localised pollution caused by untreated sewage and other wastes. The pollution of ground water which produces one-quarter of our total water supply is increasing also and there are fears that many sources can never again be restored even if the pollution ceases.

Generally speaking, domestic and industrial wastes cause most of the damage but in recent years, agriculture has become a very serious polluter. Raw animal slurry and silage effluent get washed into streams and lakes while the heavy use of fertiliser is causing grave concern. Much of this leaks into the ground water supply causing irreparable damage.

One of the anomalies in regard to water pollution is that the local authorities, who are the administrators of the law, are in some cases the worst polluters, releasing large quantities of untreated sewage into local waters. Very often this is due to lack of money for the erection of treatment plants but there is a general feeling that despite limited resources matters could be improved considerably if the will to do so were there.

Air pollution: Economic damage from air pollution is extremely difficult to quantify but it is estimated that damage to human health is the major component though there are also damages to buildings and in some instances to agriculture through animal deaths.

Most of Ireland is fortunate in enjoying relatively pure air and in having avoided the extreme experiences of more industrialised countries. Nevertheless, air pollution levels in Dublin have reached threshold levels in respect to human health and are getting worse as a result of the recent shift from oil to coal burning. Lead emissions from car exhausts are also causing concern. Air pollutants can and do produce fatalities, particularly among the populations subgroups at risk, the very young, the old and the long-term effects of relatively low pollution levels on the population generally. Exposure to fairly small concentrations of sulphur dioxide and other noxious substances over an extended period is considered to be strongly associated with the increased frequency of chest and heart complaints in recent years.

Hence in regard to air pollution and to the environment generally the motto must be 'eternal vigilance' on the part of the people. But in any anti-pollution campaign there are responsibilities to be kept in mind also. We need industrial growth badly and it must not be jeopardised by scare stories regarding potential pollution which may not occur. Each case must be treated fairly on its merits.

PEOPLE

No discussion of natural resources would be complete without reference to our most important resource — our people. But like all resources people are a raw material which must be organised and trained for the work they have to do. I quote from Robert Kane who in 1845 said 'the labouring force of man must be considered as lying truly dormant so far as its true uses are concerned until it be quickened by the energetic fire of industrial education' and going on he said 'It is in this regard that Ireland is actually weakest and that most difficulty may be expected in any future of our industry'. We have, or course, advanced considerably since those days and particularly since the early 1960s but so also has the rest of the world and we still lag behind in many ways. There is a lot of catching up to be done if our natural resources are to be fully developed and we are to attain acceptable levels of income and employment for our people.

6. The Growth of Government

Brendan Walsh

The expansion of the Irish public sector during the 1960s and 1970s was spectacular. The number of activities undertaken by the state and the amount of money spent on them increased dramatically. The share of taxation and public spending in GNP doubled over these two decades. By the early 1980s, Sweden, Denmark and the Netherlands were the only western countries in which the public sector was larger than in Ireland (OECD, 1985).

This transformation of Ireland into one of the most socialised countries outside the centrally planned economies did not come about as a result of a conscious strategy. Nothing in the intellectual climate of the late 1950s would have led us to anticipate the explosive growth of the public sector that was to occur in the two following decades. The Irish Catholic hierarchy were very hostile to any measures that could be interpreted as socialist. Their preference for 'voluntarism' over 'bureaucracy' led them to oppose the extension of state activity or control in areas such as health and education. The welfare state was condemned because the philosophy behind it conflicted with that contained in Papal Encyclicals. Economic planning was suspect because of its intellectual links with the atheistic communist states in eastern Europe.

The mood of the administrative and financial establishment was equally hostile to the expansion of the state's rôle in the economy. The Department of Finance document *Economic Development* published in 1958 and subsequently credited with an important rôle in the economic recovery of the 1960s, took the view that the size of the public sector, and spending for current purposes in particular, was already excessive. It was stated that:

> High taxation is one of the greatest impediments to economic progress because of its adverse effects on savings and on enterprise ... High taxation is necessitated by high expenditure and can be reduced only if expenditure is reduced ...

In order to make it possible to give the economy 'the tonic of a significant reduction in taxes on incomes, profits and savings', unproductive public sector expenditure should be curbed and resources set free for productive private enterprise. While seeing an important rôle for the state in promoting productive investment, and an urgent need to plan state spending more systematically, *The First Programme for Economic Development* covering the period 1958-62 envisaged an overall reduction in the rôle of the state in the country's economic affairs. The main thrust of this programme was to try to switch state spending from 'unproductive' categories such as social services and subsidies to households to 'productive' purposes such as infrastructure investment and subsidies to enterprises, while reducing the overall level of taxation and public spending. Developments over the years that followed were at variance with this philosophy in terms of both the level and composition of public spending.

The ratio of central and local government taxes to GNP is a readily understood and relatively reliable index of the importance of the public sector in the national economy. The change in this ratio over time illustrates the dramatic growth of the Irish public sector. At the end of the 1950s taxes came to just over 20% of Ireland's GNP. By 1973 this ratio had risen to 31% and by 1985 to 42%. Even more dramatic has been the growth of taxes on income, from 6% of GNP in 1960 to 23% in 1985. At the beginning of this period, an industrial worker on average earnings would not have been liable to income tax at all, but today a single man could have over two-thirds of any overtime earnings or bonus payments taken in PAYE and PRSI.

Another measure of the growth of the public sector is provided by the proportion of the economy's total consumption consisting of public sector consumption, that is mainly the wages and salaries of those who work in the public sector. In 1960 about £1 in every £7 of consumption expenditure consisted of public sector consumption; this has risen to £1 in every £4 in 1985. A quarter of all the final output of the economy now consists of the services provided by public sector employees. Most categories of public consumption have grown rapidly, with expenditure on health and education displaying the most striking rates of increase. Public sector current subsidies and transfer payments have also grown very rapidly, from 9% of GNP in 1960 to 21% today. The magnitude of these payments by the state to housholds is often overlooked by those who lament the burden of taxation on households. In fact the amount collected through taxes on the incomes of households is almost exactly the same as the amount returned to them by way of transfer payments. However, the public is much more conscious of the former than of the latter.

The public sector also plays an important rôle in investment spending in Ireland. About one-fifth of total investment consists of direct public sector investment, that is the construction of roads, houses, and other publicly owned capital structures. This share has remained fairly stable over the past quarter of a century. There has however been a big increase in the level of capital grants to enterprises, which in 1983 equalled 10% of the total private capital spending. The amount now spent on this type of aid to business is equal to over 85% of the amount collected from the corporation tax.

Since 1973 public spending has grown more rapidly than the revenue from taxation. The gap has been closed by increased borrowing, much of it from foreign sources. Until the 1970s the convention of not borrowing for current or day-to-day expenses was religiously observed, but by the middle of the decade the Irish public sector had become heavily dependent on borrowing to finance current spending. As a consequence, the public sector has become a major absorber of net national savings, instead of a net contributor to the total as was the case in the past. In the early 1980s the public sector's dissavings amounted to over one half of the total savings of the private sector of the economy. This enormous appetite for funds made it imperative to borrow abroad in order to maintain the availability of credit to the private sector. Thus the high level of public spending not only caused a high level of taxation but also led to the accumulation of foreign debt that now amounts to over £8 billion. More than £800 million is now being paid in national debt interest to foreigners each year.

The legacy of past borrowing will make it more difficult to balance the books in the immediate future. The revenue from taxes is sufficient to meet the cost of current spending when interest payments on the national debt are left out of the account. The trouble is that debt service will cost over £2 billion this year, which amounts to over 40% to total tax revenue. If we continue to borrow at the present rate, the ratio of interest payments to national income will continue to rise.

Statistics alone are not adequate to convey the extent to which the rôle of the public sector in Irish life has increased over the past quarter of a century. Behind the statistics lies a major extension of the functions and rôle of the state. The traditional view that the state is only responsible for providing a narrow range of essential services that would not be provided by private enterprise, for maintaining a framework within which individuals can pursue their economic self-interest, and aiding the weakest members of society who are not reached by voluntary charity, was replaced during the 1960s and 1970s by the view that the state should assume a much broader range of responsibilities. Major new commitments were entered into in the fields of education, health and housing. The state's rôle in the development of the economy was greatly increased. It accepted new responsibilities for social policy and the distribution of income. The concept of poverty was broadened to the point where over a third of the population were classified as poor and the social welfare system was seen as responsible for alleviating this state of affairs. Somewhat inconsistently, the dependence of a large proportion of the population on state benefits is now cited as evidence of the failue of policies in this area. A climate of opinion developed in which it seemed progressive to identify an unmet need and to demand with indignation that the state spend money on it. Politicians responded to this mood by competing in their promises to spend public money. The link between increased public spending and the ever-rising burden of taxation was not clearly perceived.

A proliferation of new state agencies during the 1960s and 1970s was the most colourful manifestation of the growth of the public sector. About forty new state-sponsored bodies were created, with responsibilities ranging from the promotion of Irish firms to the prevention of fires, from the rescue of ailing industries to the improvement of the public's health. Money was spent on an unprecedented scale to promote industry, agriculture, fisheries, industrial training, economic, social and medical research, the arts, overseas development, the Irish language, sport, livestock breeding ... In fact, it is difficult to think of an activity that is not eligible for one if not several types of state grant or tax concession. The success of some pressure groups in obtaining support inevitably prompted others to emulate them in seeking state aid. This process has led to a diversification of energy from real business to lobbying for state support.

The creation of a myriad of new agencies has obvious drawbacks. The smaller agencies have high overheads and a significant proportion of the money allocated to some projects is absorbed by the expenses of running the agencies set up to administer them. The size and complexity of the larger agencies makes them autonomous empires ruled by executives who although paid from public moneys are not directly answerable to the elected representatives of the people. Public sector bodies that fail to perform the tasks they were created to discharge have not been closed down. Agencies that have successfully done the job for which they were established remain in existence long after they have outlived their usefulness. Although some amalgamations and rationalisations have ocurred over the years, until Irish Shipping Limited was liquidated, no state-sponsored body has been closed in the entire history of the state.

Several factors contributed to the climate of opinion that fostered the growth of the Irish public sector over these years. We were influenced by international developments and the fact that the public sector was expanding in all western European economies. The sustained economic growth that occurred during the 1960s was viewed as an opportunity for closing some of the gap that existed between Ireland and her neighbours in the level of spending on health, education, housing and social welfare. The example of the British welfare state was very influential in Irish intellectual circles. It was widely believed that the only way to achieve adequate standards in many areas was by providing services free or at a heavily subsidised price through the public sector. Ireland's entry into the European Economic Community offered another opportunity for 'catching up' and was used as an occasion for raising the level of spending on social services. It was even hoped that equality between the Irish and British levels of social spending would help to solve the Northern Ireland crisis by making it easier for the northern majority to accept a united Ireland!

The growth of the public sector was also facilitated by the erosion of traditional social teaching of the Catholic Church, which viewed the welfare state as socialist, and socialism as a percursor of atheistic communism. By the 1970s several bishops were arguing that the state had a duty to use the tax and social welfare system to tackle the poverty and inequality that were widespread in Ireland. The nature of the Irish political process, in which political parties compete in their promises to the electorate, rather than offering them opposing economic philosophies, contributed to the growth of public spending while making it difficult to increase taxes at the rate required to finance this spending. Only the commentaries emanating from the

Central Bank of Ireland and the Department of Finance maintained a consistent opposition to the growth of public spending and borrowing. This verbal opposition was not, however, backed up with effective controls. Indeed these parts of the public sector themselves shared in the general expansion that they deplored!

The economic crisis of the mid-1970s abruptly changed the environment within which western democratic governments were operating. Sustained economic growth could no longer be relied on to generate buoyant tax revenues from which ever-increasing public expenditure could be financed. However, this fact was not quickly appreciated by the general public, which continued to look to the politicians to maintain living standards. In Ireland, this was very evident during the 1977 general election. The manifesto that brought the Fianna Fáil party to power in 1977 committed the new government to major tax costs and increased public spending. The sharp increase in borrowing required to finance these measures was viewed as a temporary expedient, required to stimulate private spending. The rate of public sector recruitment was accelerated over the period 1977-81 and the number employed in the public sector grew to an annual average rate of 3.3% (Humphreys, 1983, Table 52). No moderation in public sector pay has been forthcoming in return for this spurt of job creation. The public sector wage bill increased at an alarming rate, leading inevitably to hefty increases in the burden of taxation. This has provoked massive protest and unrest in which public sector employees have played an important rôle.

At the end of the 1970s, when, if things had gone according to plan, the private sector should have begun to take up the running, unemployment increased sharply and real incomes fell. The level of public spending continued to grow at a time when revenue buoyancy fell sharply. Increased borrowing provided a temporary palliative and sustained living standards for a while, but eventually raised the level of indebtedness to the point where the growth in interest payments became a major obstacle to restoring order to the public finances.

As the public finances deteriorated to the point where it was no longer possible to increase the level of spending through higher levels of borrowing, discontent with falling living standards led to an all-party consensus on the need to reduce or at least stabilise the level of taxation. Awareness increased that schemes such as 'free' education and 'free' transport are in fact tax-financed. Politicans became more aware that votes can be lost through unsound use of tax-payers' money, but it remains to be seen whether this new realism will survive an election campaign.

Another factor that had changed the environment for the public sector is the growing scepticism regarding the ability to fulfil many of the promises made in the past by the proponents of increased spending. Social scientists have expressed disappointment with the results of the unprecedented expansion of spending on health, education, social welfare and housing during the post-war period. Marked inequalities persist between social groups and the poorest classes still experience absolute deprivation despite the proliferation of programmes whose aim was to eliminate poverty and inequality. In economics, the dominance of Keynesian ideas had declined. Assessments of the net contribution of increased government spending or borrowing to the growth of output in a small open economy have been scaled down. The fact that unemployment rose sharply in Ireland at the end of a decade when public sector exployment expanded from 23% to 29% of the total number at work has undermined confidence in the belief that a continuation of the strategy pursued during the late 1970s would lead to full employment. The stagnation of employment in industry despite two decades of intensive state assistance to this sector has generated widespread unease about our reliance on state grants to foster industrial development. Even the enormous infusion of taxpayers' money into agriculture after our entry in to the EEC did little to alleviate the structural problems of under-development and poverty in this sector.

While there are some who cite these failures in support of the case for an intensification of the state's rôle in the economy, other have concluded that they demonstrate the state's limited competence in many areas where it assumed commitments during the post-war years. This would point to the need for greater selectivity in state programmes as part of a general strategy of reducing the level of spending in order to bring the public finances into order and eventually reduce the level of taxation.

Attitudes towards the public sector have also been influenced by an apparent decline in its ability to respond to shifting public preferences. There is evidence of this in the growth of spending on private sector substitutes for services that are provided by the public sector, such as broadcasting, security and policing, inter-city bus transport and mail delivery. Many reasons may be given for this development. Public sector organisations are inflexible. The absence of a profit motive tends to engender a lack of responsiveness to the changing realities of the market place. The appropriate mix of public and private sector enterprise has also been affected by changes in technology. Reduced entry costs have ended the inevitability of a state monopoly in areas such as broadcasting and telecommunications. The examples of deregulation and privatisation in other countries are being used to illustrate that there are alternatives to the model that we in Ireland espoused during the post-war period.

However, despite the rather dramatic changes that have occurred in the economic and intellectual climate, there has not been a sudden reduction in the level of government spending, nor is this likely to occur in the immediate future. There is a wider consensus about the general need to prune public spending than about the specifics of how this should be done. We still lag behind most western European countries in the level of provision of many public services, and neither the public nor the politicians are willing to accept that we simply cannot afford the standards that have been achieved by our richer neighbours. Wasteful public spending is not readily eliminated. Those who benefit from £1 of public spending will fight for its retention even if its real value to them is less than £1. Some public sector activities are sustained not because of the services they provide but because of the employment at stake. With unemployment as high as it is today there is an understandable reluctance to shed superfluous workers or close down uneconomic activities, even if it is hard to justify the amounts that are spent per job maintained in some loss-making public enterprises.

The present government is committed to a process of reversing the growth of public spending. The strategy by which this is to be achieved was set out in the national economic plan, *Building on Reaility,* published in October 1984. The objective for the period 1985-1987 is to stabilise the shares of public spending and taxation in GNP. This implies continuing to borrow to pay for approximately one-quarter of government current spending. The amount borrowed for capital purposes will fall as spending on new electricity generating capacity and telecommunications equipment tapers off. However, the level of public indebtedness will continue to increase more rapidly than GNP, so that the ratio of national debt interest payments to GNP will continue to increase. Thus even if the corrective measures outlined in the plan are successfully implemented our public finances will remain in an unstable condition.

Even the modest targets set out in this plan are proving difficult to achieve. The attempt to impose discipline on public spending has proved politically harmful and has not been pursued with sufficient determination to prevent a gap from emerging between the Plan's targets and the out-turn, particularly in the area of public sector pay. Present indications are that this gap will become a chasm during 1986. While recent reductions in interest rates and in the value of the American dollar have improved the budgetary prospects for 1986, higher than expected levels of unemployment and public sector pay could more than offset these favourable developments and require additional expenditure cuts if the government's basic economic strategy is not to be abandoned.

The temptation to abandon the attempts to restore order to the public finances will increase as the opportune moment for a general election approaches. It is to be hoped that this time round the public will realise that while some temporary relief from the malaise that affects our economy would be obtained by pursuing soft options, such as strategy would only postpone the difficult decisions that have yet to be taken in order to undo the harm that has been caused by the excessive growth of public spending during the past quarter of a century.

7. Living Standards

Peter Cassells

The 1960s and the 1970s were the best times but they were also the worst of times. In the past twenty-five years, living standards have improved substantially in Ireland. There was an almost universal increase in incomes, the decline in population was halted, social welfare payments improved in real terms, free eduation was introduced and expenditure on housing and health services increased.

Yet by the end of the 1970s, our living standards still lagged behind those of most of our European neighbours. Indeed, in the period 1960-85, with the exception of Britain, the gap between Irish living standards and those of other EEC countries widened. Today, living standards in other EEC countries are between twice and three times the Irish. Prices soared in the 1970s, urban/rural tensions developed and poverty had not been eradicated. Dissatisfaction with the tax system was manifested in a variety of ways such as PAYE marches and the growth of the black economy. The growing cost of unemployment and the burden of financing government borrowing has meant, in recent years, a general depression of living standards.

So, what *really* happened to our living standards? Who got rich as a result of economic development? To what extent was poverty ameliorated? Why was there little consensus in the 1970s about how the problems facing the Irish economy should be tackled?

Ireland was transformed in the 1960s and 1970s. Industrialisation, the 'prime mover' of the improvement in living standards was taking place against a back-drop of changing attitudes, values and structures in Irish society. This change made a welcome contrast to the relative stagnation of the previous decade. In the 1950s, people in Europe were experiencing a rapid increase in their standard of living due to high productivity levels, the welfare state and the consistent commitment by governments to full employment. Ireland did not share in this economic expansion. In the last five years of the 1950s nearly a quarter of a million men and women left Ireland convinced it had no future. In comparative terms, the wage levels of those who remained behind were low. In 1960, nearly 6 out of 10 Irish industrial workers earned less than £10 per week, while in Britain the figure was less than one in ten.

With rising unemployment, emigration and falling living standards, Ireland's ability to continue as a viable economic and social entity was in question . Dr Whitaker, Secretary of the Department of Finance at the time, summed it all up as follows:

After thirty-five years of native government people are asking whether we can achieve an acceptable degree of economic progress. The common talk among parents in the towns, as in rural Ireland, is of their children having to emigrate as soon as their education was completed, in order to be sure of a reasonable livelihood.

Then came the sudden shift to economic growth after 1960, which brought for many an unprecedented increase in living standards. The growth rate of output, which is one indication of that increase, was, in the period 1961-73, more than double previous rates. Another indication is personal income after tax. Correcting for prices changes it doubled over the twenty-three years between 1957 to 1980.

In the 1960s a lot of emphasis was placed by government and by trade unions and employers on the need to improve living standards. The First Programme for Economic Expansion (1958) was introduced to improve Ireland's capacity to progress economically 'at the rate needed to give all who want to live in Ireland an acceptable income'. The Second Programme (1963) claimed that 'the increased resources made available by this programme will make possible a significant improvement in living standards'. The National Industrial Economic Council, in a major report on full employment, stated that the objective of their proposals was the 'attainment of full employment at a standard of living which will be acceptable to the community and which will improve in line with standards in Europe generally'. There was, however, as we shall see later, little agreement on what constituted an acceptable standard of living and the relationship between different kinds of incomes.

Up to 1960, the prospects of the family business or farm was, for the majority of people, the major influence on living standards. In the 1960s, however, there was a dramatic change in the structure of the labour force as people moved away from agriculture and self-employment into industry and services. By the mid-1970s, the dominant factors in determining a person's living standards were educational qualifications, the job obtained with those qualifications and the earnings from that job.

Irish statistics on earnings and the distribution of income are very deficient. From the figures available, however, we know that the earnings of workers increased substantially. The average weekly earnings of a male worker in 1960 in Player Wills, for example, was £10 for a 47-hour week. The executive officer in the civil service, a position which with national teaching or a place in university was much sought after by the bright boys and girls from rural Ireland, was paid, on average, £15 a week. Dr Ken Whitaker, who as Secretary of the Department of Finance is credited with Seán Lemass for the boom in the Irish economy in the 1960s, was paid £60 a week.

Today the average earnings of the male industrial workers are nineteen times higher at £200 for a 43-hour week. For the executive officer in the civil service, they are twelve times higher at an average of £180 a week but they now earn less than the average male industrial worker. The salary of Dr Whitaker's successor, whose job it is to advice on the relaunching of the Irish economy in the 1980s, is also twelve times higher at £700 a week. But as I will show prices also increased in this period.

In the 1960s women received lower increases than men and, until the equal pay legislation of 1974, were paid less for doing the same job as a man. The earnings of women in industry, while low, improved, however, from 55% of male average hourly industrial earnings in 1960 to 68% in 1984. The earnings available to families also improved with the growth in two-income households, as more and more married women, particularly in the 1970s, returned or remained in employment.

Very little is known about low paid workers in Ireland and whether their position relative to other workers has improved. Side by side with the new industries and new services of modern Ireland, there continued the 'dead end' jobs, with relatively little increase over time in real earnings, no fringe beneifits such as an occupational pension, poor promotion prospects and a higher than average rate of job vacancy. Many of these jobs are in the traditional sectors of the Irish economy, for example, clothing, footwear and agricultural workers, and services such as hairdressing, catering, contract cleaning and law clerks. Joint labour committees were established to set down minimum rates of pay for these areas. There were attempts in the pay rounds of the 1960s and in the National Wage Agreements of the 1970s, to improve the position of the lower-paid by flat rate increases and minimum payments. Most of the evidence available would suggest, however, that where differentials were eroded, they were restored later by special agreements.

A reduction in the working week and more annual holidays means an increase in leisure which should be counted as an increase in living standards. This period saw the establishment of the 40-hour week but only after a three-month strike in the building industry in Dublin in 1964. There was also an increase in the minimum holiday period from two weeks to three weeks, with most workers by 1985 enjoying 20 days' annual leave. Between 1960 and 1985, however, the average hours worked by adult males in industry fell by only four hours from 47 to 43, a relatively small decline over a period of twenty-five years. This tendency to work long hours for more money income is explicable given relative earnings in Ireland compared to other countries, the small number of multi-earner households compares with other countries and the larger family size in Ireland.

An improvement in living standards was also enjoyed by farmers. Having increased slowly in the 1960s Irish farm incomes grew rapidly in the early and mid-1970s, then declined and began to recover again in the past few years. How did the farmer's income increase compared with the earnings of the industrial worker? In the 1960s, the farmer's income which varies of course by farm size, was about 80% of the gross earnings of the industrial worker. With the very rapid increases by the 1970s, farm earnings actually exceeded industrial earnings in 1973, 1977 and 1978.

The rapid improvement in farm incomes in the 1970s induced a dramatic increase in capital investment, as farmers bought farm machinery, erected farm buildings and bid up the price of land on borrowed money. New houses and larger cars also appeared and the flask and sandwiches at half-time at Croke Park were abandoned for the steak and onions in the Clarence Hotel on the way home. The continual denial by farm leaders of this obvious improvement in incomes and their rejection of every proposed scheme to tax that income, led to major tensions between farmers and people in the neighbouring towns and cities, where the majority of the population now lived.

Much of the improvement was due to agricultural price increases and adjustments in the green pound rather than increased output, so that today the same questions are raised about agriculture as were raised in the First Programme for Economic Expansion (1958) — the extent of unutilised agricultural land; the variability in economic performance and farm incomes among different categories of farmers; the rigidities of the land-tenure system.

For many people in Ireland, their standard of living is dependent on social welfare. About one-third of the people as compared with one-fifth in the 1960s, receive weekly social welfare payments. With improved payments, increased eligibility and the introduction of new schemes, expenditure on social welfare doubled in the 1970s as a percentage of GNP. Since 1979, there has been a narrowing of the gap between incomes of some social welfare households and the net income of those at work, particularly in the cases of widows and old age pensioners. Despite these improvements many social welfare recipients are still living on a mere subsistence. Today a typical family — husband, wife and three children — dependent on unemployment assistance has a maximum income equivalent to only one-third of average male industrial earnings. Indeed, the dramatic increase in unemployment from 90,000 in 1979 to over 225,000 in 1985 and the increase in the duration of unemployment, has had an enormous impact on living standards, particularly from working class families. The fact that one-in-three heads of working class households are now without a job will have an enormous impact on their future living standards and those of their children.

So far we have seen an increase in the incomes of most workers, farmers and some of those dependent on social welfare. But economic growth does not occur in an even spread. Left to itself, it tends to widen the gap between the rich and the poor. Despite the relatively rapid economic growth achieved in the 1960s, the extent of poverty is still considerable. In the 1960s it was widely believed that poverty would soon be eliminated and inequalities in Irish society reduced. By the early 1970s reports were showing, however, that at least one-quarter of the population were living below the poverty line. Conferences on poverty were organised, a National Committee on Pilot Schemes to Combat Poverty was established and abolished, and books were published on the one million poor.

Left to itself, economic growth also widens the gap between rich places and poor places. It is striking, therefore, that in Ireland income per person appears to have grown at a fairly uniform rate in all four provinces. A measure of success has been achieved in improving the living standards in the less developed areas in the country and the gap between Leinster and Connacht has actually narrowed. The focus of attention has now switched to deprived areas within cities, such as Dublin, Cork and Limerick. A 1979 study found that many inner city workers depend upon jobs in short-life industries which provide them with low incomes and very limited prospects in the long term.

Living standards are strongly influenced not only by pay but also by related variables, such as prices, taxation and government expenditure on transfers and the social programmes. One of the features of the period since 1960 has been the vast acceleration in the rate of price inflation. In the decade 1970-80, the average rate of increase in consumer prices was over 15% per annum, as against 5% for 1960-70. This rapid acceleration in inflation reduced living standards and also redistributed income in highly arbitrary ways, creating whole new classes of poor.

There has also been a big rise in public expenditure. This increased expenditure can be regarded as an improvement in the social wage, in the form of higher pensions and a greater volume of state services, but in Ireland it is not often percieved in this manner. The beneficiaries of this increased public expenditure were not always the most needy. Indeed, in the case of some forms of expenditure, the rich had their living standards improved more than proportionately.

Expenditure on education, which increased rapidly in the 1960s, overwhelmingly benefited the better-off. Studies show that nearly half of the children of unskilled workers still leave school with no qualifications, compared with only 1 in 20 of the children of the self-employed. Three-quarters of the children of doctors, solicitors, substantial farmers and employers, for example, enrol in third-level institutions. The chances, however, of a child from an unskilled manual background graduating from a university are some five times less than their chances of 'graduating' from a psychiatric hospital. The most revealing thing from these studies of the social class backgrounds of second-level and third-level students is that there has been virtually no change over the last twenty-five years.

There has also been a phenomenal increase in expenditure on the health services since 1960. Most of this expenditure improved the health care and the health status of the rich more than the poor. An extraordinary range of housing subsidies to encourage owner-occupation was introduced. These subsidies ensured that above average-income households now have the highest quality housing.

The distribution of the tax burden is just as important as public expenditure in determining living standards. Over the past twenty-five years there was a very substantial increase in the overall tax burden and very substantial changes in the composition of tax revenue. The share of income tax and social insurance contributions in total taxation rose significantly, with a large decline in the share of corporation, capital, wealth and property taxes.

Following the recommendations of a Commission on Income Taxation, established in 1957, some changes were introduced in the tax system, such as Pay As You Earn, in the 1960s. But it was the changes in the system made in the 1970s and the decline in the real value of personal tax allowances that most affected living standards and the redistribution of income.

Attempts were made from 1974 onwards to gradually extend income tax for farmers. These were resisted and a farm levy, a resource tax and agricultural rates were abolished. Estates duties were replaced; a wealth tax was also abolished in 1978 following pressure from powerful individuals. Rates on private homes were removed rather than reformed and taxes on companies were reduced. The net effect of these changes was to reduce the tax contribution of property owners, the wealthy and companies, with income tax payers absorbing the reduced burden.

High levels of inflation in the 1970s also resulted in significant shifts in the tax burden. The failure to adjust tax allowances and tax bands for inflation meant there was a steady movement of low-income families into the tax net and that individuals paid tax on a greater proportion of their incomes and at higher rates than hitherto.

Analysis of whose living standards were improved or reduced as a result of all these changes, shows that employers, owners of wholesale and retail services and farmers substantially improved their relative position. They also benefited most from the combined effect of taxation and public expenditure. Salary and wage earners, whether manual or non-manual suffered a significant and essentially equal increase in their tax burden. Middle-income households with young children fared least well. Since 1979, however, the aver-

age tax rates of single people increased substantially. The poor suffered most from the high level of indirect taxation. A growing proportion of income escaped the tax net with the increase in the black
economy which has now become known as the golden economy.

The shift in the burden of taxation and the ability of certain powerful groups to have specific taxes abolished, became a source of
increasing friction between different sections of the communtiy with
a quarter of a million people taking to the streets in 1979 to protest.
Another Commission on Taxation was established.

So, who gained from the economic changes of the past twenty-
five years in Ireland? In most countries, occupations, privilege and
prestige change from one generation to another. Recent ESRI
reports show that while improvements in standards of living have
been almost universally experienced in Ireland since 1960, the differentials between the top and the bottom of the class structure
remain. Access to the peak of the class hierarchy in Ireland, where
living standards are highest, is, unlike many other European countries, severely restricted. Those who had large-scale property holdings or professional qualifications in the 1950s were able to secure a
comparable level of advantage for their children in the 1960s and
1970s either through inheritance or their virtual monopoly of the
advantages that depend on education. Shop-keepers and other self-
employed persons improved their position over the bank clerk and
the bus conductor. The gap between those who were paid a salary
and those who were paid a wage narrowed. But in this whole process, the poor became more marginalised, in particular because of
the high level of unemployment.

This picture of living standards in Ireland pieced together from
the facts and figures on incomes, taxation and public expenditure
does not show the underlying tensions and discontent in Irish society about these issues.

As a country we are now faced with enormous problems which
have no easy answers and have major implications for our living
standards in the future. Thousands of jobs will have to be created
just to prevent unemployment from rising further. The substantial
borrowing from abroad, which made possible the increase in living
standards in the mid-1970s, will have to be serviced and ultimately
repaid. Increases in expenditure will be required simply to maintain
present levels of services given the evolving demographic structure.
Unless there is a substantial increase in economic growth, then little

or no increase in real personal incomes is likely to occur.

If we are to successfully tackle these problems then we must learn a number of lessons from the tensions and conflict of the 1960s and 1970s.

The oil crisis of 1973 and the subsequent world recession led to a slow-down in the pace of improvement in living standards, but there was little consensus about how the burden should be shared. Instead, there was intensified competition at all levels of Irish society to defend or enhance relative positions. There was also a feeling in some quarters that, as in *My Fair Lady,* the rich were still having fun, but the poor got the blame.

This was not new. In the 1960s there was no consensus either about the manner in which increases in national output should be shared between persons and different sections of the community. In 1967, the NIEC pointed out that 'whatever past consensus there may have been on the relationship between different categories of incomes has weakened'. They speculated in the language of tripartite bodies that 'this may be as a result of changing views on what constitutes an acceptable degree of inequality in the personal distribution of incomes ... together with a feeling that some categories may at times escape their fair share of direct taxation'. In 1971, Dr Kieran Kennedy suggested that 'the substantial upward shift in wage demands may be an expression of profound dissatisfaction with the existing distribution of income and wealth'. As we have seen, however, little was done during this period, in particular by governmental tax and expenditure policies, to redistribute income and wealth.

The lesson we should learn from the 1960s and 1970s is that the current crisis in the Irish economy cannot be resolved unless we increase the national cake. Economic growth will improve the prospects for job creation and reduce the imbalance in the public finances far faster than further cuts in public expenditure or increases in taxation. Developmental policies to increase the national cake will not win the active support of a majority of the community, however, if they do not tackle the inequalities in income, in educational opportunities and in our taxation system.

Policies for income moderation will not be accepted unless they cover all incomes, with specific and effective controls on incomes from self-employment, trading profits and rental income. Measures will have to be introduced to guarantee workers that moderation in income increases would be directly translated into jobs. Also as the recent Telesis Report pointed out, no country has successfully achieved high incomes without a strong base of indigenously-owned resources or manufacturing companies in traded (i.e., exporting) businesses. These incidentally are lessons that some small countries, with significantlly higher living standards, such as Austria, Denmark and Finland, have already learned.

Finally, if the mistaken policies of Ireland in the mid-1950s are not to be repeated, we should heed the advice of that emminent economist Patrick Lynch 'that policy-making must draw from different disciplines, not merely from the economist, whose importance has often, perhaps, been exaggerated'.

8. Class and Social Mobility

Christopher T. Whelan

In Ireland class distinctions are thought of as typically English phenomena. The popular impression is that rigid social class demarcation was left behind with the ending of landlordism and the demise of the Anglo-Irish ascendancy. It is certainly true that class boundaries in Ireland are less ritualised, or less marked by cultural differences, than elsewhere. This has encouraged the notion that we are a classless society. The late Roy Geary, a distinguished director of The Economic and Social Research Institute, was fond of wryly noting that there are no classes in Ireland, because we are all descended from the high kings of Tara. My task is, the rather unenviable one, of arguing that class barriers in Ireland are substantially more rigid than in countries such as England.

'Class', as I intend to use the term, does not necessarily imply snobbishness or deference. I have in mind something more pervasive and fundamental. Classes are made up of people whose occupations are similar in terms of their sources and levels of income, their degree of economic security, their chances of economic advancement and their degree of autonomy in performing work tasks and roles.[1] It might be asked what insight is gained by applying class labels to such differences. In using the term 'class', I am seeking to draw attention to the way in which inequalities feed off each other to create distinctive life styles. Class groups share not just economic positions but a web of social relationships, attitudes and values. We are dealing with, not merely sets of people carrying out similar jobs, but definite social groups with a recognisable identity.

I would like to develop this point by looking at the consequences of inequalities in work experience. A great deal of work is organised in a manner which minimises opportunities for the use of skills. Methods of control or supervision are chosen so as to eliminate the uncertainty arising from the exercise of choice by workers. Many jobs are designed in a fashion that makes them more suitable for the mentally handicapped than the average worker.[2] The work situation has a dual significance, not only may certain kinds of labour be dehumanising, but habitual exposure to such conditions stultifies the worker's capabilities to be flexible, sensitive and creative in other areas of his life.[3] Research in Ireland has shown that unskilled manual workers are least likely to develop the kind of leisure activities, and relationships between work and home lives, which allow for the full enjoyment of retirement.[4] Deprivations at work are not compensated for by life outside the work situation. Instead, they spill over into relations between workers and their families. We are dealing with the 'hidden injuries of class'.[5]

It is not only work experiences which contribute to the creation of social classes characterised by distinctive life styles. The emergence of such groups is, mainly due to the absence of kinship, friendship and neighbourhood ties across the lines of class division. The lack of such ties is, in turn, a consequence of barriers to class mobility, both across generations, and within the individual's work life. Housing segregation is an outcome, not simply of urbanisaton, but of the influence of class on consumer behaviour and housing policies.

Class groups obviously differ in the amount of money they have. They also differ in the extent to which society allows them to take advantage of available rewards and avoid deprivations. I will use the phrase 'life chances' to refer the opportunities people have of sharing in the economic or cultural goods which exist in the society.[6] Of course, life chances vary by class in the more literal sense. The relatively favourable health situation enjoyed by professional and managerial workers is not accounted for solely by income and work environment influences. Life style factors relating to, among other things, diet and cigarette smoking play a significant part. The superior educational performance of their children is, at least in part, due to parental aspirations and support. It is the reality of distinctive life styles which make class distinctions as valuable to the marketing practitioner as the sociological theorist.

If we are still uncomfortable thinking about Irish society in class terms, perhaps it is because the extent to which the social structure has changed over the past thirty years has not been fully grasped. In 1951 almost half the work-force were employers or self-employed. The majority were in agriculture. For the children of these individuals life chances depended on their prospects of inheriting the family business. Education could secure a livelihood for only a minority of the work-force. Inequalities of opportunity were reflected in emigration. Of those born between 1936 and 1941, by 1961 only 3 in every 5 remained in Ireland. The class structure today reflects the selective process of emigration to Britain of young men and women from small farms, farm labouring, and unskilled manual backgrounds.[7]

By the mid-1970s wage bargaining, in a class system, containing sharp distinctions by skills and qualifications, became the dominant factor in determining life chances.[8] To all appearances, meritocracy triumphed over inheritances and nepotism. What matters now, it seems, is not who a man is but what he can do. Futhermore, what he can do is judged by criteria which are open to inspection. The elimination of inequalities of opportunity which arise from inherited differences, has been a central objective of social policy.[9] I will seek to show that, in fact, there has been a remarkable stability in the distribution of privilege. To achieve this it will be necessary to examine the evidence on patterns of social mobility in Ireland. In so doing one is confronted with the fact the available evidence is far from ideal. There are problems relating to the time at which data were collected, geographical restrictions, the exclusion of females, and the absence of class data for certain educational transitions. However, despite such difficulties, I hope to convince you that a consistent and relatively unambiguous picture emerges.

The most comprehensive evidence on social mobility in Ireland comes from the early 1970s.[10] At that time, movement between social classes was much less prevalent in this country than in England, France and Sweden. This conclusion holds even when one allows for differences in the kind of jobs available in the countries covered by mobility studies. One might expect substantial changes to have occurred since then, in view of the transformation of education since the late 1960s. However, when we have considered the evidence, I think you will agree that, while the changes constitute a considerable achievement, their impact on mobility chances has been a good deal less marked than most people would believe.

Let us deal first with the evidence relating to the early 1970s. The degree of movement and stability that we observe depends on the number and type of social classes identified. In what follows, I will concentrate on mobility which can be unambiguously labelled as 'upward' or 'downward'. Three major classes are distinguished:

(i) The 'professional and managerial class' which includes employers and large farmers;

(ii) 'the immediate non-manual class' with whom non-agricultural self-employed and medium sized farmers are comparable; and

(iii) 'the manual class' together with small farmers who have equivalent life chances.

Using this classification, it becomes clear that social class is far from fixed at birth. In the early 1970s, almost 1 in 2 males had experienced mobility across these class boundaries over the generations. People are not born to succeed or doomed to failure. Of course, what most people want to know is how frequent or rare is movement from rags to riches. However, since the amount of mobility we observe depends on the number of classes we identify, rags, riches and rarity, like beauty, lie in the eye of the beholder. What we can say is that only 1 in 20 moved from manual origins to the professional and managerial class while a mere 2% of those with fathers in the latter class were currently in manual work. Movement from rags to riches is rarer than movement from rags to relative affluence, but a great deal more common than movement from riches to rags.[11]

Equating high levels of mobility with equality of opportunity, turns out to be simplistic. Sons of professional and managerial workers were themselves six times more likely than the sons of manual workers to be found in the professional and managerial class. They were also six times less likely to be in manual work. International comparisons show that the magnitude of these inequalities is much greater in Ireland than elsewhere.[12]

The pattern of social mobility in industrial societies is a consequence of underlying inequalities of opportunity, and changes in the occupational structure which create room at the top. Even when we allow for such differences, the degree of inequality of opportunity in Ireland was remarkably high by international standards. Tendencies towards immobility were consistently stronger in Ireland than in the other countries. Restrictions or long-range mobility were also more powerful. On a scale of 'openness', Swedish society lay at one extreme and Ireland at the other.[13]

This conclusion is consistent with the evidence that, in the early 1970s in Ireland, social class had a very strong influence on educational achievement. Education, in turn, played a crucially important part in influencing life changes in Ireland because of the low level of career mobility.[14] In the intervening years the significance of educational qualifications has increased. However, we might expect that the developments in the educational system in the last twenty years would have altered the relationship between class background and educational achievement. The series of far-reaching educational reforms, begun in the 1960s, which included the abolition of fees for post-primary education, had as a key aim the reduction of educational inequalities.

The Irish educational system has expanded dramatically over the past twenty years. The number of 15 year olds still at school increased from less than half to over 85% between 1965 and 1979. Over a similar period, the number of males doing the leaving certificate rose from just over 1 in 5 of each age group to just under half. By 1979 1 in 5 entered a third-level institution.[15] It might appear that such an expansion of educational participation must lead to a reduction in educational inequalities and increased social mobility. It is necessary, however, to distinguish between the total proportions achieving particular levels of schooling and the impact of class background on educational achievement. We cannot ignore the extent to which the percentage who fail to reach particular levels are selected from the bottom of the class hierarchy. This point can be illustrated by reference to the National Manpower Services surveys of school leavers between 1980-1982; these surveys show that, while 8% of male pupils left without any qualification, the figures varied from less than 1% of the upper non-manual group to 18% of the unskilled or semi-skilled manual group.[16] The degree to which differences in educational outcomes are related to class origins remains disturbing.

At second level, it has been estimated that boys from upper non-manual families are at least six times more likely to sit for the leaving certificate than are those whose father is an unskilled or semi-skilled manual worker. Furthermore, they are almost thirteen times more likely to enter third-level education.[17]

What are the consequences of educational inequalities of the kind we have been considering? If we take unemployment, we find that the rate is three times higher for those who left school before sitting for any public examination. Likewise, among those who do find employment, the better jobs go to those with higher qualifications.[18] In Ireland, as elsewhere, there is little evidence that increasing the percentage participating at higher levels of the edualtional system, in itself, serves to reduce class-based educational inequalities.

With the decline in self-employment and the spread of bureaucracy and a meritocratic ideology, the long-run trend in industrial societies has been away from patronage, nepotism and direct inheritance of positions. Still, the struggle between social groups for scarce opportunities, most emphatically goes on; it has simply moved to a new arena. The game is increasingly played through strategies of child rearing refereed by the schools and the examination system.[19] It is inequalities in 'competition' for places in the educational systems which are crucial in determining the distribution of occupational opportunities. The value of a qualification, such as the leaving certificate, does not remain constant in a period where the number obtaining the qualification expands dramatically. One example of 'qualification inflation' in the educational requirements for jobs is that, with the recent decline in clerical employment opportunities, post-leaving certificate school leavers have moved into those areas previously dominated by early school leavers, particularly manual and service work. Similarly, the proportion of apprenticeships taken by school leavers had declined, as increasing numbers of post-leaving certificate school leavers have come to take up the available apprenticeships.[20] Until recently, school leavers without qualifications were also least likely to be offered places on either AnCO training or Work Experience Programmes.[21] The Youth Employment Agency has responded to the problem of the low level of penetration of youth programmes among those with the most severe problems by giving priority to young people who have been unemployed for over six months, and by expanding programmes which are particularly tailored to the needs of the less qualified.[22] Occupational positions are passed from one generation to another not, as in the past, through direct inheritance but through the medium of differential access to educational qualifications. The educational inequalities I have described show that it remains inheritance with a vengeance.

Recommendations that expenditure be redistributed in favour of the primary sector stem from a recognition that class differences in educational attainment emerge at an early age. There is evidence of striking differences in verbal ability by the age of 11.[23] Evidence of this sort led many to the conclusion that the working class family environment is culturally *deprived,* in that it provides inadequate conditions for the development of cognitive skills. This interpretation has been challenged by those who maintain that such environments are culturally *different,* providing effective conditions for the development of abilities that differ from middle class definitions of intelligence and desirable behaviour. What is at issue is not the judgement , in any absolute terms, of working class culture as 'good' or 'bad' but the possibility of a discrepancy between working class attitudes and values and those required for success at school.

In Ireland, at present, the solution to such problems is being sought mainly through specific intervention measures aimed at helping those pupils identified as disadvantaged. The 'Programme for Action in Education 1984-1987' proposed that in addition to giving priority of funding to primary schools, special support will be given to those primary schools which cater for a high proportion of children who are disadvantaged in respect of social and educational background. [24]

None of my subsequent comments is intended to detract from the need for, and the value of, initiatives which have intended to assist the most educationally deprived. It has been estimated that almost 11% of each age group in the early 1980s left school before the legal minimum age of fifteen. Annual surveys of school leavers carried out by the National Manpower Service indicate that some 10% of each year's group of school leavers leave post-primary education without having sat for any public examination. [25]

I must stress though that the relationships between social origins, ability and achievement in the Irish educational system show that we are not confronted simply with a minority of disadvantaged children and schools who have obvious social problems. We must face the wider problem posed by the vast majority of working class children who achieve well below their potential. Specific programmes for the disadvantaged school will not have a major impact on this wider problem. Class barriers which lead to under-achievement do not disappear as one moved through the system. Progress through the second-level system, and to third-level education, is far from being on the basis of ability alone. I am not arguing that there is a conspiracy to exclude working class children from these parts of the educational system. Obviously, the operation of the points system ensures that third-level places are allocated among applicants on the basis of performance. However, the class composition of third-level students is not entirely a consequence of the pool of students eligible to seek entry. [26] The odds of leaving certificate school leavers entering the labour market, rather than continuing on to third level are two-and-a-half times greater for those from upper non-manual backgrounds, even when performance in the leaving certificate is taken into account.[27] Failure to adequately acknowledge the importance of such inequalities encourages the erroneous notion that our post-primary schools and colleges have a very limited potential to contribute to the reduction of class differentials. Substantial non-meritocratic elements are involved in the allocation of pupils to different sectors of the post-primary system, in determining their prospects of survival within the system, and their chances of going on to third level.[28] Such differences cannot be plausibly explained solely by reference to class differences in aspiration. Differences in commitment to education by parents and pupils are a contributory factor. But we cannot stop our search for explanation at this point. We must go on to ask how such attitudes are produced by social conditions.

We should avoid concluding that educational inequalities are caused by factors beyond the scope of public policy. In this regard, we should not neglect the manner in which the educational system is organised. A good deal of work is in progress on the possibility of curricular reform. It is also important that we should understand the effect of competition between sectors, selective admission arrangements, and procedures for differentiating between pupils within schools, such as streaming. Very sharp differences exist between the intake of secondary and vocational schools. Among pupils doing the intermediate certificate, we find that vocational schools cater mainly for working class and small farm pupils, who make up two-thirds of their intake. Secondary schools are predominantly middle class, particularly for boys, while the class composition of the newer community and comprehensive schools is more balanced.[29] Corresponding to these social class differences among schools are equivalent differences in the concentration of educational and social problems. Estimates by school principals suggest that over 1 in 7 of school entrants had serious numeracy and literacy problems in two-thirds of vocational schools, one half of community schools, and less than a quarter of secondary schools. Part of the explanation lies in the class composition of pupil intake in the three types of schools. However, there is a strongly held belief among the staff of vocational schools that stiff competition exists for the more academically able working class pupils, and that, by and large, they suffer badly from such 'creaming off' practices.[30]

In addition to applying selective admission criteria, some schools rigidly stream their pupil intake with a clear hierarchy of classes on the basis of assessed ability. They then discriminate amongst these classes in terms of their subject type and level. The rigid streaming of classes has been shown elsewhere to have an adverse effect on the educational achievement and levels of self confidence of those assigned to lower ability groups.

What conclusions can be drawn from the evidence we have reviewed? There is clearly a great deal of social mobility in Ireland. The scale of change in the occupational structure in the past thirty years makes that inevitable. However, the degree of inequality of opportunity is high by international standards. For every working class lad or lassie 'made good' there are many more who have been denied the opportunity to develop their talents to the full. Unless we believe that society has no need of such contributions, the waste of talent involved is regrettable, not just from the standpoint of the individual but from a societal perspective. A rigid class structure has implications for efficiency and social order. Worker-management relationships in Ireland are characterised by high levels of distrust. The extent of this distrust is related to the fact that the groups involved have little in common in terms of their social origins or current life styles.[31].

Rather than contributing to the destruction of class barriers, the educational system has acted to ensure a remarkable stability in the distribution of privilege. One of the paradoxes of a free society is that privileged groups retain the freedom to fight in protection of their privilege. In order to achieve a situation of equality of opportunity we would have to remove the association between class background and educational achievement. Perfect mobility, in the sense that one's class destination may be independent of one's origin, may, therefore, be impossible to achieve without severing the ties between the child and his family almost completely. Such extreme measures are neither practicable nor desirable. However, what comparative analysis of mobility patterns shows is that it is possible to come a good deal nearer the target of equality of opportunity than has so far been achieved in Ireland. Considerable progress on this front should, therefore, be possible.

An important obstacle to progress, however, is that while the state is responsible for educational expenditure it has relatively limited control over educational outcomes. The class composition of second-level schools is, largely, an outcome of decisions taken by private institutions. We lack bodies such as local education authorities which would integrate the efforts of all types of schools in dealing with the problems and prospects of children in their catchment areas.

If, however, the existing inequalities are viewed as intractable, then it is important that we do not hide behind an unsustainable defence of our educational system as a meritocratic one. If we accept the inevitability of the class nature of the educational system, then its function in providing a means by which scarce occupational opportunities may be distributed should be acknowledged. In that case it would be appropriate to pursue the more modest goal of assisting the particularly disadvantaged through specific programmes. However, in such circumstances it would seem reasonable that those for whose benefit the system operates should bear a much greater share of the costs.

9. The Family in Transition

Finola Kennedy [1]

A hundred years ago in rural Ireland land ownership largely determined whether marriages took place and whether families were established. After the Famine the subdivision of holdings almost ceased, and as there were few jobs available other than on the land, the opportunities for marriage were restricted. The trend of emigration was already well established when the pattern of late marriages and celibacy emerged. Given the strength of family ties and the extension of rural ways of life into the towns, similar patterns appeared in urban life. Irish society, at the turn of the century, was based on the denial to many of its members of the opportunity to found a home and family in their native surroundings.

Little apparently had changed by the 1930s when the American anthropologists, Arensberg and Kimball, carried out their classic study in Co. Clare. [2] For the Irish countryman the family had a certain priority over the individual. Keeping the family farm intact for the heir often involved a mixture of emigration and postponement of marriage for other family members. Within the family there was a rigid division of labour, with authority and decision-making resting in the father, while the emotional focus of the family was the mother.

By the end of the 1940s when another American, a Jesuit sociologist, Alexander Humphreys, studied rural migrants to Dublin, he found 'The New Dubliners' were adapting their family life to the changed cultural matrix of the city. [3] The familiar urban division, between the male world of work and the female world of home and family, evoked the same kind of changes in rôles and organisation, as had occurred in urban families elsewhere. In the late 1960s whenDamian Hannan carried out a study in Co. Leitrim, [4] he found that family-centred values, so dominant in Co. Clare in the 1930s, had faded.

THE CHANGES

Since the 1960s the patterns of the traditional rural family have been coloured by the definite markers of the urban family. The younger age at marriage, the longer formal schooling of the partners, the sharp drop in the fertility of marriage, the greater likelihood of married women in employment, the increased incidence of family breakdown, the greater involvement of government in the family, may even be reckoned so significant as to constitute distinctly new patterns.

For several generations Irish society was characterised by late marriages and by a high proportion of the population who never married. In the 1960s the old moulds were finally broken. Marriage rates had been rising since 1951, and in the improved economic conditions of the 1960s, accelerated rapidly after 1966. In the past ten years, however, the number of marriages has been falling.

During the 1960s and 1970s the number of births rose fairly steadily, but there has been a truly dramatic decline in the last four years. Total births rose from 61,000 in 1960 to a peak for this century of 74,000 in 1980, but then fell by 10,000 to 64,000 in 1984. What is even more remarkable is the fall in the number of legitimate births. In four years legitimate births declined by over one-sixth. Births to married women, that is, marital fertility, have fallen significantly since 1961, with the biggest fall in the older age groups. The average number of children per completed family in 1981 was three compared with four a decade earlier. Twenty years ago there were over 200,000 children in families of six or more children, compared with less than half that number at present.

In Ireland, there are no comprehensive data on either family breakdown, or cohabitation, which are widespread features in other developed economies. The Joint Oireachtas Committee on Marital Breakdown and Labour Force Survey data both suggest that several thousand persons are involved in marriage breakdown. Information is available on one important aspect of sexual activity outside marriage, that is the number of births to unmarried mothers. In 1984 over 5,000 babies were born to unmarried mothers, a five-fold increase since 1960. One in twelve births is now to an unmarried mother. Nearly all adopted children in Ireland are illegitimate. In 1960 adoptions were equivalent to one half the number of illegitimate births, compared with less than one quarter at present. The decrease in adoptions relative to illegitimate births must be due in part to the increased number of unmarried mothers who keep their babies. There are indications that, despite social welfare support, many single mothers experience great, and often overwhelming, difficulty in coping with their situation. In 1981, for example, over one-third of the total number of children admitted into care were admitted because their unmarried mothers could not cope.

Not all pregnancies end in the natural way. The number of Irish women availing themselves of facilities for abortion in England since the 1967 Abortion Act has risen from a handful to 4,000 in 1984. Four in every five abortions are performed on single women, mainly young single women.

The improved economic conditions of the 1960s which enabled more people to marry and at a younger age, provided other opportunities also. Marriage partners in the 1980s have more formal schooling than their counterparts in the 1960s. Combined with better education, improved job opportunities enabled more women to find employment, while changes in employment conditions led to an increase in the number of women who kept their jobs after marriage. Although still low by international standards, the labour force participation of married women, particularly of young married women, has been rising rapidly. In 1984, however, the labour force participation of married women aged over thirty-five actually fell. This probably reflects the lack of labour market opportunities, given the very high level of unemployment. Today one in five married women belongs to the labour force compared with one in twenty in 1961. This trend marks a significant shift from the traditional 'bread-winner father' situation. It is reflected, for example, in mortgage provisions which take account of the wife's earnings.

Many changes have been made in conditions governing women's employment, in particular following Irish entry to the EEC, which facilitated the growth in the employment of married women. Chief among the early changes was the removal of the ban on married women teachers in national schools in 1958. This crucial change came partly in response to a shortage of teachers. But it was also influenced by arguments put forward in the *Report of the Commission on Emigration* about the effects on family formation of increased employment opportunities for women. Echoing the 1937 Constitution, the Emigration Commission deplored the possibility that economic necessity might force a married woman to go out to work. Still, as the Commission remarked in a practical way, if a woman could keep her job after marriage, the extra income might facilitate earlier marriage and give a sense of greater security. The Commission expressed the view that the removal of the marriage ban in the civil service, in the banks, and for teachers — all of which in turn came to pass — would help to raise the marriage rate.

The labour force participation of married women has grown despite the relentless climb in unemployment. Unemployment threatens the stability of many families. About one-half of the long-term unemployed in Ireland have family responsibilities and the average number of dependants is between three and four.

In addition to the legislative changes which affected the employment conditions of married women, an important group of laws was enacted in the past few decades which affected rights of married persons to the ownership and inheritance of property. These include *The Married Women's Status Act (1957)* which permitted married women to sue in their own right and to be sued; *The Succession Act (1965)* which set limits on the extent to which a surviving spouse and children might be disinherited; and *The Family Home Protection Act (1976)* which prevents either spouse from disposing of the family home without the written consent of the other. In three important instances, major changes affecting the family followed from court cases taken by private individuals — Mrs Magee, Mrs Airey and Mr and Mrs Murphy. The judgments in these cases led respectively to changes in the law on contraception, in the state's duty to provide free legal aid in family law cases, and in the tax treatment of married couples.

It is not only, or even primarily, through changes in the law that the state has influenced family life. From maternity services to death grants the state affects family welfare from cradle to grave. Traditionally, the old age pension eased the handing over of the family farm to the heir. Arensberg and Kimball observed: 'There is no chance that the old people would give up the land but for the pension, and there is no hurrying them'. [5]

The three main 'forms of government financial recognition of families with dependent children are allowances under the Income Tax Code, Social Welfare Children's Allowances, and payments for child dependants of social welfare recipients. In a nutshell, the trend in these three categories of state support for families has been the elimination of the child tax allowance, and the maintenance in line with inflation of the Social Welfare Children's Allowances and the child dependant allowances. Since the late 1960s, a continuous decline occurred in the child tax allowance compared with both the allowance for a married couple and the allowance for a single person, until its complete abolition in 1986. From the viewpoint of those liable to income taxation, the late 1960s were the halcyon days for the family.

The changes which have taken place have tended to bring the Irish family into line with the family in other developed countries. The trends now in operation point to an even closer convergence. For example, Ireland now has one of the fastest declining rates of marital fertility in Europe. If this continues, family size in Ireland will conform to the European norm. The increased participation of married women in the work force and the growth of government involvement in family life are well documented throughout the developed world. With certain key exceptions, such as divorce, which must reflect in part the legal position, Ireland fits the general pattern.

WHY HAVE THE CHANGES TAKEN PLACE?

Some of the reasons for the changes in the Irish family are similar to those in the countries whose patterns Ireland has followed. Two facets of industrialisation — urbanisation and technological change — are widely regarded as major causes of change in family patterns. With urbanisation, the family sheds its economic focus as a production unit, while technological advance has replaced labour in the home, by means of domestic appliances, convenience foods and disposable nappies. One result of technological change has been to free housewives from many labour intensive chores, while a related consequence has been a huge fall in domestic service employment over a long period. The development of the Welfare State has absorbed many tasks previously undertaken almost exclusively by family members, such as care of the aged. In the case of birth itself, there has been an almost total move away from home births towards hospital confinements.

The penetration of cultural influences from abroad provides part of the explanation of change. The general opening up to the wider world which started with the Free Trade initiatives of the 1960s gathered momentum after Irish entry into the EEC in 1973. The widespread upsurge in foreign travel highlighted Irish awareness of life in foreign climes. The influence of the media was certainly considerable. The development of RTE in addition to the availability of external channels helped to hasten change. The television set replaced the fireside as the focal point of many homes. The *Late Late Show* and Gay Byrne opened many a previously closed book. For example, it was on the *Late Late Show* that an unmarried mother was first enabled to explain her situation directly to the Irish people. The *Women Today* programme dealt with topics which were previously taboo. The women's pages in the newspapers carried less about cookery and more about changing lifestyles.

The Women's Movement, which developed in Ireland in the 1970s, with its emphasis on individual fulfilment, was in tune with the individualistic values of economic growth which had been fostered from the late 1950s. Some of the most significant changes for the family were also most significant for women. One aspect of the Women's Movement encouraged women to reduce their child-bearing, increase their labour force participation and further assert their independence.

The growth in population in the 1960s, following decades of population decline, led to a change in attitudes towards population growth and, by implication, childbearing. For several decades, population had been the central fact to which everything in social and in economic life was referred.[6] The persistent decline in population up to the 1960s had touched national pride at a vulnerable point and even called into question the merits of self-government. A major change was recorded in the late 1970s when, in response to a request to the Irish government from the United Nations, for a choice of option concerning the natural increase of population, the government registered a change in attitude. The governments of a number of countries, including Finland, Greece and Ireland, which up to then favoured higher rates of natural increases, shifted to the view that current rates were satisfactory.

In the changed economic and social environment of the past two and a half decades there has been a shift away from that set of values, enshrined in the Constitution, which regarded the rôle of the woman in the home as the primary rôle to be cherished and protected, towards a set of values which is more labour-force oriented. This change in emphasis is illustrated forcefully by the major document produced by the Working Party on Women's Affairs and Family Law Reform early in 1985. The Report focuses on the changes 'associated with more and younger married women in our popula-

the home. The majority of mothers then and now are not in the labour force. In this respect Browne's efforts could be interpreted as supporting the constitutional ideal. Yet is was bitterly opposed.

The shift away from the traditional family in which authority and decision-making rested predominantly with the father, and the emotional support with the mother, combined with a rigid sex-based division of labour between the partners, towards a more modern family in which there is greater sharing in child-rearing and household tasks may be an enriching experience for both men and women.

Some observers of 'The Family in Transition' will view the efforts to eliminate all aspects of sex stereotyping as a mistaken attempt to gloss over, even to deny, the essential complementarity between men and women. Some will signal a danger that the continued trends of labour market participation by women could result in extremely low fertility or in numbers of children receiving doubtfully adequate care. Views will differ on the increased role of the state in family affairs. Some argue that state social benefits and services can undermine the family unit by robbing it of independence and responsibility. The contrary view is that the family can only flourish and fully carry out its responsibilities if it receives adequate support from the state in the form of income support and help with the education of children, caring for sick and disabled members and so on. Many will see virtue in elements of both sets of arguments and will be interested more in the balance between state support of family rôles and responsibilities.

Looking to the future, further changes are pending. Although the referendum to remove the constitutional ban on divorce was decisively defeated, some changes in marriage laws may be expected. The government has promised to abolish the legal concept of illegitimacy. The full effects of the wider availability of contraceptives are as yet unclear. Legislation is being prepared to give the state more authority to place children in care. The economy is severely depressed. Jobs, which must be the economic cornerstone for many marriages, are scarce. Social welfare payments now provide the basic income for many families from the moment of marriage. The marriage rate is falling rapidly. Whatever the future may hold for the Irish family, however narrowly or widely defined, experience of the years 1960-1985 suggests that the family in Ireland has been borne along on the tide of developments in the more economically advanced countries of the world. In so far as it ever existed, the separate identity of the Irish family is no longer recognisable.

10. Crime and the Criminal Justice System

David B. Rottman

INTRODUCTION

Crime, criminals and prisons are unavoidable images when we think about the state of Irish society in the mid-1980s. Their prominence is one measure of the distance that separates the Ireland of twenty-five years ago from Ireland today. Twenty-five years ago crime was something that afflicted other countries. Today, fear of becoming a crime victim is a feature of daily life that affects nearly all of us. For many, it is also a symptom of something that has gone terribly wrong with Ireland and its people. Crime is to the 1980s what emigration was to the 1950s: a mark of the nation's failings.

I would certainly argue that crime has evolved in response to the economic and social changes that this country experienced over recent decades. But I believe that the relationship is more complex than is often appreciated. I also believe that the extent of the increase in the crime problem was not inevitable. Some of the damage can be attributed to bad policy choices made by successive governments.

I begin with a brief chronology of criminal activity since 1960 and then turn to post-1960 developments in the criminal justice system. Having offered a description of what occurred, I offer an explanation as to why crime has changed so dramatically in recent years and why the criminal justice system has been so ineffectual in responding. Finally, I turn to what can be done to reduce the level and seriousness of crime.

CRIME TRENDS

Criminal activity in 1960 was at a level far below that in most European countries. It had been so almost continuously since the immediate aftermath of the civil war. A brief upward trend during Second World War was the exception, but it was not sustained. Such crime as did take place was unsophisticated in execution, non-violent in consequences, and rarely profitable. Crime was attributable to a small band of rather untalented repeat offenders, more often resident in prison than practising their vocation. Here, too, the exception in the form of renewed IRA activity was sporadic and did not leave a durable impact on the nature of crime. The chief legacy, instead, was the separate legal apparatus provided in the Offences Against the State Act of 1939 to cope with the threat from subversives.

There was obvious public concern over crime in 1960, but it focused on the 'Teddy-Boy' phenomenon, an imported fad. Like all fads, it soon passed into memory, having posed a minor threat to public decorum rather than to life, limb, or property.

The mid-1960s brought a decisive break with the old pattern. From 1964, large annual increases were recorded in the official statistics on the number of property offences such as burglary, robbery and car theft. The rise was unrelenting. Between 1964 and 1975, burglaries grew 4.3-fold in frequency and robbery 11.4-fold. Over the same years the average value of property stolen in burglaries doubled (taking inflation into account). Assaultive offences such as murder also increased, but at less than half the pace for property offences.[1]

The upward trend slowed in the late 1970s. However, it was then that we can first observe change towards greater diversity, skill, sophistication, and profitability in criminal activity. This was most apparent in the use of firearms in robberies. Armed robberies in that period cost the lives of five gardaí and eight bystanders.

This change in method was consolidated in the present decade. Such a change in the nature of crime is more important than the resumption of the upward trend in offence numbers. The more business-like character to crime was soon much in the news through the scandal of a substantial drug abuse problem in Dublin. But the change was also generally evident in major property offences such as burglary. Some of that change was directly due to an overspilling of the Northern Ireland problem into the Republic. But the more permanent effect may prove to have been indirect. Groups not involved in the conflict imitated the methods and weaponry of subversives. Though limited to a relatively small proportion of all offenders, this effect had a substantial influence on the nature of crime in the Republic, one that will outlast more fleeting manifestations such as 'joyriding'.

One consistency across the decades has been the characteristics of the person most likely to become involved in crime. That person is young, male, unemployed, without educational qualifications or skills, and from the most economically deprived areas of Irish cities. [2] The point is not that such a combination of characteristics makes crime either inevitable or in any sense excusable. Rather, social disadvantage increases the probability that persons will become involved in crime, will persist in such activity, and end up guests of the nation's taxpayers in prison.

How serious is the crime problem today? The garda crime statistics are not a reliable yardstick for answering that question. Police statistics refer to a number of offences of which they are aware. Though they can indicate long-term shifts in direction, such as those I have outlined, the difference between the number of offences 'known' this year compared to last year has no significance. [3] Public concern over crime and police efficiency vary from year to year and affect the amount of crime that is officially known.

Fortunately, in the 1980s we can refer to another way of measuring the problem: crime victimisation surveys. Such surveys ask a large number of randomly selected families whether they had been the victim of various criminal offences in a given time period. If they had, details are obtained on the number of incidents, the loss sustained, and whether the police were notified. In 1982-1983 the ESRI surveyed some 9,000 adults for that purpose. The results check the comprehensiveness of the garda statistics and provide a profile of the persons and houholds most at risk of becoming crime victims.

The ESRI survey was the first of its kind in this country. We cannot, therefore, use its findings to re-assess the conclusions drawn from the official statistics about recent trends in crime. Such an exercise proved illuminating in other countries. Change over time in public willingness to report crime incidents and modifications to police book-keeping practices often account for much of the increase registered in police statistics.

Since we lack a time dimension for evaluating our victimisation survey, I adopt the situation in other countries as the standard for comparison. The British Crime Surveys of 1982 and 1984 offer a particularly relevant standard for assessing Ireland's crime problem.

Ireland's position in 1983 can be summarised as follows:
Viewed comparatively, the rates of burglary and car theft are higher in Ireland than in either England or Scotland. [4] The difference can

be expressed in terms of incidents per 10,000 households: 450 of every 10,000 Irish households were victims of burglaries and 562 of a vehicle theft. In England the rate for burglary was 260 and for vehicle theft, 232. Scottish rates were almost identical to those in England (257 and 280). Most other forms of property crime, however, such as thefts from vehicles and vandalism, were not more common here than in Britain. We also know from international comparisons based on official statistics that violent crimes such as murder remain infrequent by British and continental European standards.

What is extraordinary about crime in Ireland is the extent to which it is concentrated in Dublin. Crime rates in other cities such as Limerick, Cork, Galway and Waterford are less than half that of Dublin, a rate that is found in all urban places, including large towns. Crime victimisation for the 57% of the population who live outside of cities (places of less than 10,000 population) is so infrequent as to be negligible. One way of expressing the difference is another comparison with Britain. The average inner city London resident bears five times more risk of becoming a burglary victim than someone living in rural England. A person living in Dublin's inner city has twelve times the risk borne by a resident of rural Ireland.

Even within Dublin, the risk of crime victimisation is far from evenly shared. The typical household victim is sited near the city centre, relatively well-off and unprotected. Generally, the ESRI Survey suggests that fear of crime is more widespread than the actual risk of becoming a crime victim.

It also indicates that Irish crime victims are more likely than British victims to report incidents to the police. The contrast is particularly striking for minor property offences. People here set a lower standard in deciding what is a 'crime' than is the case in countries where high crime rates have been present for some time. High reporting rates may also, of course, reflect higher confidence in the police.

THE CRIMINAL JUSTICE SYSTEM IN TRANSITION

Such co-operation, let alone confidence, indicates quite dramatic developments in the field of criminal justice since the foundation of the state. Ireland on Independence, inherited from Britain a set of Victorian and Edwardian institutional arrangements for law enforcement — police, courts, and prisons — and a tradition of mistrust between citizen and state. Much was retained from that inheritance. The decades of low crime levels provided little incentive for reform or innovation. [5] Therefore, in 1960 the machinery available for enforcing the criminal law was one fixed for the needs of a crime situation that had already faded into history generations earlier.

Two pre-Independence legacies are of particular importance. First, Irish criminal law is antiquated and unconsolidated, as are many of the procedures governing investigation, prosecution, trial, and sentencing. Second, the criminal justice system lacks cohesion. Specific agencies like the garda síochána are highly centralised in their own command structure, but there is little co-ordination between agencies at the centre. One result is that responsibility for making vital decisions is not clearly allocated.

The challenge of rising crime levels quickly revealed the system's inadequacies. It was in the garda síochána that the first stirrings of a response to modern conditions occurred. A process of consolidation was under-way throughout the 1960s, leading to the closure of many of the smallest rural stations. Motorised patrols were introduced at the same time in cities, along with the communication and investigation technology of modern policing. The opening of the Training Centre at Templemore indicated the prevailing commitment to greater professionalism, while the inauguration of the Juvenile Liaison Officer Scheme testifies to the willingness of experiment.

The force also began to look outward to enlist public support. *Garda Patrol* went on the air in 1965. The next year's *Report on Crime* included, for the first time, a section describing crime prevention efforts. The setting up in 1968 of the Conroy Commission raised expectations that fundamental reform would follow. But although the Conroy Report led to a final break with the quasi-military tradition inherited from the Royal Irish Constabulary, the political will is still lacking to tackle the structural problems the Report identified, notably vagueness in the force's relationship to the Department of Justice. Politicians preferred to put their faith in numbers. The force expanded from 6,600 in 1960 to 11,400 today. The dead hand of nineteenth century administrative practise still prevails. Meanwhile, the rise in the level of crime was paralleled by a decline in the arrest rate for major property crimes to about one-half of what it had been in 1960. [6]

Some important bureaucratic changes did emerge elsewhere. The Probation and Welfare Service was established in 1961 as a distinct agency within the Department of Justice. It now supervises all probation orders and prepares all pre-sentencing reports for the courts. In 1974 the prosecution function was also given a separate existence. The Director of Public Prosecutions (DPP) took over the rôle previously assumed by the Attorney General of bringing criminal charges before the jury courts or the Special Criminal Court. The decision on whether to prosecute was thus effectively insulated from extra-legal considerations but no basis has been found to make the DPP's office the nerve centre for the state's strategy on specific cases.

With the 1970s it was the turn of the prison system to enter the modern era. Specialised institutions such as the Training Unit and the Open Centres were established and the commitment to education and rehabilitation greatly expanded. A sensible programme of planned, supervised early releases was implemented. By 1985 this progress was largely reversed. Ireland's prisons became so overcrowded as to force the abandonment of improvements introduced at great effort and expense over a 15-year period.

The criminal justice system today operates in a legal climate quite different from that of 1960. Innovations made early in the history of the state had consequences which remained largely dormant until the 1960s brought out their potential. A written Constitution was the most important of these. In Ireland, unlike Britain, the Constitution states basic principles which have precedence over all legislation. The judiciary has the responsibility of ensuring that legislation and administrative practice comply with the Constitution, which incorporates a bill of individual rights.

This break from the British model had implications that were fully realised only after 1960 when Irish lawyers discovered that the Constitution was a legal document. [7] A series of Supreme Court decisions changed the ground rules for criminal prosecutions by interpreting the Constitution as granting, for example, rights to legal representation and bail.

This growth in the use of judicial review was accelerated by the post-Independence innovation of quarantining subversive offences and offenders into a separate set of legal procedures and institutions. That innovation was given a new impetus after 1968 when the criminal justice system was confronted with the offshoots of the

Northern Ireland conflict. That led to the re-activation, in May, 1972, of the Special Criminal Court, which sits without a jury, under the Constitutional provision that special courts could be established by law when 'the ordinary courts are inadequate to secure the effective administration of justice, and the preservation of public peace and order'. This, in effect, establishes procedures and institutions designed to facilitate the processing of one type of offences and offenders, while at the same time preserving the integrity of the 'regular' legal process. It is an artificial distinction that poses grave problems for a society which adheres to the principles of the rule of law. [8] Indeed, commentators such as Bryan McMahon (1985, p.45) described this country as now having two systems of justice.

Such duality might have been intended by various governments but the judiciary has, since 1972, increasingly applied basic common law standards to cases involving subversive offences and defendants. The procedures and decisions of the Special Criminal Court do not, in practice, today differ greatly from the ordinary courts.

However, the ordinary courts are themselves increasingly in crisis: the District Court in 1924 took over from the magistrates a wide jurisdiction to try cases summarily — that is, by a Justice sitting without a jury. Modern legislation has extended that jurisdiction, particularly when the defendant pleads guilty. The burden of rising case-loads since the 1960s has, therefore, fallen mainly on the District Court rather than on the higher courts where juries reach verdicts. The court system depends on the willingness of defendants to trade-off, on the one hand, their Constitutional right to a jury trial, against, on the other hand, the limited sentencing power of the non-jury courts. The trade-off is sufficiently attractive that only four of every one hundred defendants so entitled or liable are returned for trial before a jury court. [9]

This leaves the courts the least changed of all parts of the criminal justice system. Their sentencing options have been increased with Community Service Orders and Treatment Orders for drug abusers, but the courts have been largely sheltered from the winds of change that they themselves did so much to encourage since 1960.

SOCIETAL CHANGE, CRIME, AND CRIMINAL JUSTICE

Two questions cry out for an answer when we reflect on the experience of the last quarter century:

First, why has the level of crime risen so consistently over the period? Second, why has the criminal justice system proved so ineffectual in responding, despite massive inflows of resources and personnel?

Taking the first question about the rapid rise in crime, it is clear that rising crime was one consequence of the post-1958 revitalisation of Irish society. It is wrong, however, to simply regard crime as the dark side of progress. Industrialisation and urbanisation are general processes of change linked with the modern era. The outcomes of those processes are shaped by each country's specific situation. In terms of criminal activity we can see two key outcomes: criminal opportunity and criminal motivation.

The timing and unrelenting pace of the upward spiral in the crime statistics indicates the important rôle played by changing opportunities for committing criminal offences. As Joe Lee (1979, p. 177) has observed, if Ireland became something of a rat race in the 1960s, the novelty was due to the lack of races to be run not to the absence or rats in 'traditional' Ireland. I agree with that observation, but note that it is the *change* in opportunities that has been the significant factor. That accounts for the qualitative shift in the nature of Irish crime, away from relatively trivial property crime of earlier periods and toward today's prevalence of car theft and burglary.

Opportunity for crime grew along with the size of the population. The ending of emigration and demographic change over the 1960s brought a rapidly growing population. More people, and particularly more young people, produce more crime even without any change in the willingness to break the law. So too would the shift from rural to urban places of residence.

Opportunities in the form of abundant, valuable and portable consumer goods are part of an explanation for the rise in the level of crime and the new criminal sophistication. But the magnitude of the change suggests that an increased willingness to take advantage of those opportunities also occurred.

Ireland in the 1950s was dominated by the old — their values and cautions. The balance shifted in the 1960s in favour of the young, who thereafter set the tone for society. It was a more enterprising and adventurous Ireland. But it was also perhaps more self-centred and even reckless. Certainly standards of conduct changed in a way that made it more likely that people would take advantage of opportunities for crime.

Standards of conduct in traditional Ireland were part of an overall system of values, a world view that was internally consistent and constantly reinforced in daily activities and in religious belief and practice. Standards were based on what we should do, on how we should behave. The focus was on moral obligations, not on prohibitions.

Standards of conduct today lack such a foundation. There are numerous prohibitions, but each must largely stand on its own. Since they are not woven into a single way of looking at society, specific standards can be more readily questioned and ignored when convenient.

In any case, industrial urban society is less dependent than traditional types of society on moral consensus for social integration. We are bound together increasingly by contractual, economic and legalistic obligations, such those found in labour contracts, mortgages, tax payments, and social welfare entitlements. Our willingness to conform to rules made in the common interest depends more and more on expectations of a return in the form of material well-being, jobs, and economic growth. [10] Moral beliefs no longer provide clear and persuasive guidelines for day-to-day conduct. Appeals for the family, community, or school system to instil moral values will be of less consequence in such a society than was previously the case. Morally based standards must now compete with those based on rational calculation and self-interest. [11]

That competition largely explains why the criminal justice system was so much more effective in 1960 than it is today. In 1960, responsibility for supervising and restraining behaviour was shared out among the family, church and local community. The gardaí and prisons formed a kind of reserve force, in place to deal with exceptional cases, not the generality of citizens. Today it is the criminal justice system that stands in the front line. We should not be astonished that is is inadequate. Public policies in other areas such as education, employment, housing and social welfare are the ones which have the potential to strengthen the attractiveness and availability of alternatives to crime.

The reality of modern Ireland is that many groups were left behind in the transition to an industrial consumer society, stranded in marginal positions from which their children have little chance of exiting. This is manifest today in the substantial social class differences among children in educational participation and employment opportunities. [12] This does not mean that most young people from disadvantaged backgrounds become involved in and remain involved in serious criminal activity. But they are more likely to do so than children raised in more privileged circumstances. Adequate social integration today requires that all are potentially able to participate fully in society and therefore have a stake in conformity. The criminal justice system cannot on its own be expected to significantly reduce the current high level of crime.

POLICY ISSUES FOR THE 1980s
Higher crime levels and an inadequate official response were consequences of the changes Ireland experienced over recent decades. I do not, however, wish to conclude as simply the bearer of bad tidings. The government intends to spend some £350 million in 1986 to protect us from crime. That provides ample scope for immediate results, if some redirections to policy are made.

The first is a more equitable distribution of resources across the agencies of the criminal justice system. Money should be allocated where it offers a potential return in the form of lower crime levels and enhanced protection from dangerous offenders for the community. The Office of the DPP, the Probation and Welfare Service, and the courts are the main candidates for such increases. Expenditure on policing in this country has already passed the point beyond which it is sensible to anticipate an additional return. The decline in arrest rates is due to inherent problems of policing widely dispersed urban areas such as Dublin. Recruiting more gardaí or introducing new investigative powers will not overcome that difficulty. A more efficient use of resources, particularly in patrol strategies and style of policing, offers potential, along with actions that maximise public co-operation with the gardaí. [13]

Second, there must be greater cohesion to criminal justice decision making. Important decisions such as to arrest, charge and prosecute are currently divided among several agencies with little co-ordination. A centralised, adequately staffed prosecutor should be the nerve centre of the state's processing of cases. Without that cohesion individuals who are guilty evade punishment and others who are not guilty are unnecessarily subjected to criminal charges. The public interest is best served by a prosecution system that adequately screens and prepares cases, thus ensuring that the full rigour of the law is applied where appropriate.

A third redirection is that proposed by the Committee of Inquiry into the Penal System (1985). The Committee advocated two basic principles: prison should be the punishment of last resort, used only for those who commit grievous offences, and the deprivation of liberty is itself the punishment. The current prison over-crowding violates those principles. It is a myth that locking offenders into prison cells is an effective way to protect the community from further injury. This obviously may apply in the case of specific offenders, but as a general policy it is counter-productive. Two-thirds of all prison sentences are for less than one year, so imprisonment buys short-term protection at a very expensive price. For many ex-prisoners, their incarceration will enhance rather than diminish the probability of re-offending. The recent experiment of allowing the prison population to swell to unprecedented numbers will, in my opinion, have undesirable long-term consequences for the community. It must be stressed that this rise was a policy choice, an abandonment of any serious effort to implement planned early releases. Put bluntly, an over-crowded prison system does not call for congratulations. It does not mean that the gardaí have become more efficient at catching criminals or the courts more efficient in selecting those offenders who merit the most severe penalty. It is instead a warning sign that there are fundamental problems at earlier stages of the system. The practice of 'shedding' prisoners, which in effect nullifies court sentences before they have even begun, is of course deplorable. But it can be avoided by well prepared and monitored programmes involving supervision. These include both non-custodial punishments and, where merited, early releases for those imprisoned. I stress that these options are likely to be more effective than present policies in decreasing the likelihood that those sentenced by the courts will subsequently re-offend.

But here we must be mindful of the limits to what a criminal justice system, however efficient, can achieve. A nineteenth century criminologist claimed that 'societies have the criminals they deserve'. [14] That is a harsh verdict on contemporary Irish society. It might be more reasonable to reiterate that the Irish criminal justice system can only operate effectively in an atmosphere that encourages the belief by young people that they have a stake in the existing social order.

11. The Two Faces of Irish Industrial Relations

Michael Fogarty

The best way to think about industrial relations in Ireland is in terms of the three stages in the history of the state.

STAGE 1 — THE TIME OF BEGINNINGS

The first was the time of new beginnings from independence to the 1950s. At the start in the 1920s there was anyway very little industry around. There were unions, mainly manual, with one or two exceptions like the bank officials, but total union membership was less than you can find in one large union today. There was collective bargaining, but at a pretty basic level on a limited range of pay and conditions, and in the civil service, for example, there was none. Management tended to be primitive and authoritarian. There was a body of industrial relations law, but inherited from Britain: it was not Irish law. And a conspicuous part of the argument about Ireland's national identity was a long and fierce debate over whether British-based unions could still be accepted in the new state, and in 1945 this split the trade union movement into two separate Congresses.

But all the time the country was learning. Industry began to develop, as with the Shannon Scheme, and the wave of new businesses after free trade was abandoned in 1932. Some of the gaps in industrial relations were filled. The civil service got its first conciliation and arbitration scheme in 1950 and teachers from 1954 onwards. Trade union membership doubled from 1945 to 1959, and in 1959 the split in the unions was also ended and the present Congress was formed. And Ireland began to develop its own industrial relations law, the Trade Union Act of 1941 tried to switch from British to American practice by using the law to sort out confusion over splinter unions and competition between unions. It proposed to give the union representing a majority of workers in any category sole bargaining rights for that category. But the end of that story was a break with British tradition of a quite different kind. The Supreme Court declared that part of the Act unconstitutional, and so established that Irish industrial law, unlike British, operates under the written Constitution and only within its limits. And another legal landmark was the Industrial Relations Act of 1946 which set up the Labour Court and all the machinery that goes with it.

STAGE II — THE ECONOMY TAKES OFF

The second stage in industrial relations was from the end of the 1950s through the 1970s. By that time the basic lessons about how to run an independent economy had been learnt, and in the First Programme for Economic Expansion Whitaker and Lemass pressed the right buttons and the economy took off. Production went up, pay went up, industry grew and replaced agriculture as the foundation of the economy, and the tide of emigration was reversed. All very satisfactory, but so far as industrial relations were concerned with important weaknesses of which we still have to take account. Industrial relations in the 1960s and 1970s had two faces, one positive and one negative, and so they still have today.

I take first what happened to management. Management in those years developed fast towards professionalism, including professionalism in industrial relations. In 1964 only the biggest manufacturing firms were likely to have personnel managers. By the beginning of the 1980s almost all those employing over 200 had at least one manager responsible for personnel, and so did most even of the smaller firms employing 100 to 200. Management style had changed as well. At the beginning of the 1970s Gorman and Molloy found that the old authoritarian style was going out and being replaced with more participation and involvement. And I can confirm all this from my own reviews in those years of industrial relations in organisations like the ESB, the banks, AnCo and RTE..

But studies at that time also showed a much less favourable side to what was happening to management. Gorman and Molloy found that new or foreign-owned companies might be picking up new management style, but older Irish companies were much slower to do so even though the new style was often a condition of commercial success. They found too much tendency to go by past practice instead of innovating, and, I quote, 'a reluctance to really involve people in the organisation' or to delegate responsibilities. Trade unionists agreed. Four out of five activists in a survey by Brian Hillery in 1970 complained about lack of information from managment, particularly about plans for company development.

Coming on to the beginning of the 1980s, the time of the Commission on Industrial Relations, the Irish Management Institute told the Commission on Industrial Relations that, and I quote again, only an 'infinitesimal' number of organisations had produced real personnel strategies. The Institute of Personnel Management said that some personnel managers were still little more than welfare officers, that line managers were often uninterested in personnel matters, and coined a splendid phrase about 'the procedural and substantive poverty of workplace industrial relations' in Ireland. When I interviewed a number of successful Irish entrepreneurs at the beginning of the 1970s, and asked them what they saw as the main reasons why others were not following in their footsteps, one of the points they made most strongly was that too many Irish managers were simply not aware of what first-class performance as understood in other industrial countries meant, in personnel management or anything else. And again trade unionists agreed. Only one in thirty of the activists in Hillery's survey thought their managers definitely 'unreasonable' in negotiations, but one in three thought that they were not even 'fairly' efficient.

You find the same sort of two-faced story when you come to the unions. Union membership went up fast in the 1960s and 1970s, by 43% from 1958 to 1978, and by the end of the 1970s Ireland had the third highest proportion of unionised employees in the European Community. That is a pretty good vote of confidence by Irish workers in their unions. Hillery's surveys of union officers and activists showed them to be hard-working men — though not many women — doing a solid job of negotiating on a widening range of conditions as well as pay, putting in a great deal of their own time, and generally in good relations with each other and with management.

But again there was another side. One problem was sectionalism. My own surveys showed again and again the difficulty of getting coherent and sustained action by union groups in the multi-union firms. Congress did its best to tackle problems like unofficial action, casual picketing, demarcations, breakaways, or disputes over representation in new firms, but with limited success, even though union activists would in principle have liked to see more done. Nine out of ten of them in Hillery's survey would have liked to see the union structure simplified and over half thought that there ought to be more discipline in the ranks. There was a lot of talk about solidarity with the low paid, but it proved to be one thing to write clauses about this into National Agreements and another to make them stick once sectional interests got to work with their own special claims.

Another problem for the unions was what you might call the arm's length syndrome. Charles McCarthy pointed out in a previous Thomas Davis Lecture the ambiguity in the unions in these years between a desire for partnership and participation and the preference of many trade union leaders for keeping bargaining at arm's length. That ambiguity was particularly important in a time of change such as Ireland has been going through since the 1960s. The Trade Union Research Unit at Oxford recently ran some studies of union influence in various countries on the introduction of new technology. The really sharp contrast which emerged was between the British unions, which like many Irish unions preferred to stay at arm's length and negotiate simply on the consequences of management decisions about new technology, and the Swedish unions which went right in from the start to work with management to influence the shape and timing of change in the design of technical systems, with detailed homework and strong technical back-up: which let them argue with managers on equal terms, and into the bargain impress them because their positive approach and sound technical suggestions often paid off for management as well. There was no doubt at the end of the day that it was the Swedish unions which had real influence and got the best results for their members.

When Hillery's surveys came out I wrote in a review that the picture they presented of trade union work in Ireland was sound and solid but also pedestrian: short on imagination and innovation. But there was one case where unions, management and the government did jointly innovate in a way which put Ireland ahead of the world, and that was the National Wage Agreement and the wider National Understandings of 1979 and 1980. Every industrial country faces the problem of keeping bargaining free and flexible, so that anomalies can be corrected and performance rewarded, yet also keeping the overall growth of pay in line with the growth of real income so as to avoid inflation. The Irish answer in the National Agreements was imaginative and for several years was at least moderately successful.

But once again we have the two faces of Irish industrial relations.

In the end the Agreements collapsed. The problems of reconciling free bargaining with overall control were never quite worked through. The public sector never got past the endless niggle between service managers, and of course unions, who for good reasons wanted flexibility, and the Department of the Public Service which for equally good reasons wanted overall control. The private sector had plenty of exhortations from the FUE, but never quite got over the problems of leapfrogging or of getting coherence between bargaining at several levels at once. The government offered concessions to encourage the National Agreements, but never put the boot in so as to get effective performance from employers and unions in return. And the important thing is to understand *why* this happened. There simply was not enough strength or continuity of purpose in the employers' organisations, the unions, or the government to make the National Agreements work as they should. Congress and the FUE are loose confederations of sectional interests, and can deliver only as much as particular interest groups within them will wear. The government could have put more backbone into the Agreements, but when Louden Ryan and Dermot Egan and I wrote a report about all this in 1981 we found it remarkably difficult to say anything tactful about what governments actually did.

There are plenty of other examples of the two faces of Irish industrial relations. Ireland's strike record, for instance, has not been particularly bad by comparison with Britain's. It just happens to be bad, like Britain's, by comparison with countries like Austria or the Netherlands or Norway or Sweden or Germany which have taken the bull by the horns and shown just how much more could be done to take the hassle out of industrial relations by reforming its procedures.

There then is the experiment with worker-directors in seven semi-state enterprises under the Worker Participation (State Enterprises) Act of 1977. That too was imaginative and in many ways well thought out, like the skilful way in which the problem of representation in multi-union businesses was solved by using the single transferable vote. Trade union directors have in fact played a constructive and co-operative part, especially in communicating information and breaking down suspicions. But again there was something missing. They could have played a still more constructive part if, as Congress originally proposed, participation at board level had been linked through to the rank and file by new systems of representation and participation below the board.

There is also the case of the law. The law has come into Irish industrial relations since the 1960s in a big way, and often in a positive way which no one would wish to reverse. I am thinking particularly of the way in which individual employees' rights have been increased in cases like dismissals and redundancy, holidays, or maternity rights and equal pay and opportunity. Even there, there is room for argument and detailed reform. Wage regulation through Joint Labour Committees is fine in principle but a real dog's breakfast in its actual present detail. But the big issue has been about using the law to improve industrial relations procedures. It *can* be used that way, and very effectively, as other countries have shown: but in Ireland there has been a head-on clash because of the gut reaction of many union leaders against using it for any such purpose, even if that purpose is approved by union members themselves. We know from a 1985 survey that seven out of ten union members would like the law to insist that a dispute be referred to the Labour Court before taking strike action, and four out of five would like it to insist on a secret ballot before a strike: but that is now how union leaders have seen it.

STAGE III — THE NEW WORLD OF THE 1980s
So, I come on to Stage III of the modern development of Ireland, which is from today on to beyond the year 2000. We still have the two faces of Irish industrial relations. How do we get out and beyond them? The first point about Stage III is that Ireland finds itself today in a new world, and not just because of the depression of the last few years. The point now is that the development stage of the Irish economy is over. The problem now, if jobs are to be created and maintained to keep pace with the rising population, is to keep an already industrialised society ahead of the competition in open markets with continual change in technology, organisation and skills. And on that problem I make four points.

First, in a world like this an enormous amount depends on getting full commitment from managers, unions and employees alike to competitive performance and their full involvement in achieving it. Management has to lead, but it is not just a question of giving managers their head. Professor Charles Carter has been arguing for what he calls 'development bargaining', under which management contracts to deliver the investment and technical or marketing measures needed for progress and job security and to share the resulting gains, and the unions in turn contract to contribute positively to this and to cut out hassle in industrial relations. I mentioned just now how Swedish unions and employers have gone for this approach, and how it has paid off for both. And I say particularly to the unions in Ireland that the message for them is clear. Get in there and bargain positively for progress, not at arm's length but with full involvement from the start in designing the technology and work organisation that make for a secure and prosperous future. And, like the Swedes or Norwegians, do the homework properly, lay on the necessary expert support, and bring all the unions in together, since in today's conditions none of them can do the job on their own. One of the problems about the unions in these islands, as the Trade Union Research Unit keeps pointing out, is that their ambitions are too limited.

Second, the Commission on Industrial Relations showed how much more might be done in Ireland to take the mess and hassle and unnecessary confrontation out of collective bargaining by improving its procedures, better use of the Labour Court, use of strike ballots, and so on. It is not a question of favouring either management or unions against the other. There is a mass of research to show that creating what is sometimes called a 'climate of predictability' in industrial relations pays off for both.

Third, it will be necessary to go back again to the problem which the National Agreements came so near to solving, keeping bargaining free and flexible and yet avoiding the danger of leapfrogging and inflation. That problem will not go away. To solve it in Irish conditions will need a bigger and more determined input by the government into bargaining than in countries which have stronger central authority in their employers' associations and union federations. But, given this, there is no reason why Ireland should not achieve as good a level of concertation on national policies for incomes and employment as other small countries like Austria, and it is essential that it should be done.

And finally, for any of these purposes, do not be afraid of using the law, as I think the government showed itself to be in its 1983 discussion document on the reform of industrial relations. There is a lesson here from Britain. I do not happen to be an admirer of the Thatcher government, but one thing I have to give them. They recognised that there are a lot of highly desirable improvements in industrial relations which the law can enforce and which will stick because they are welcome to rank and file trade unionists even if their leaders like to call them 'anti-union legislation'. And I could show from the days when Britain had a Labour government that the same proved to be true of many measures of employment legislation which at first were rejected by managers. Managers and unions are often afraid of being stuck with a rigid and unsuitable set of legal requirements, but the law does not have to operate that way. What it can and should do is to lay down for example that there must be proper agreements for information and participation and settling disputes, but to leave it to the parties to settle exactly what these agreements are to be.

And there is one point about using the law where I think that the Commission on Industrial Relations got it wrong. The traditional foundation of industrial law in these islands is the principle of so-called trade union immunities, meaning that a union will not actually find itself in court if it calls a strike or does many of the other things necessary for collective bargaining. The majority of the Commission wanted to stay with that principle. I do not. It is too negative, and a part of the British inheritance which Ireland could do without. What is needed today is a system of positive rights which directs the attention of employers and unions to the positive things that ought to be done, like development bargaining or better procedures for employee involvement. It is not enough for the law to say that you will not be shot if you do the right things in industrial relations. It needs to say much more positively that these are the things that ought to be done, and now get on and do them.

12. The Regional Dimension

M. A. G. Ó Tuathaigh

Up to the late 1950s in Ireland public discussion of regional policy, or of a regional dimension to economic growth and retardation, almost invariably meant a discussion of the special problems of areas along the west coast from Donegal to Kerry. These areas had, of course, been designated special problem areas as far back as 1891, when Arthur Balfour established the Congested Districts Board (CDB) of Connacht to improve living standards in areas along the west coast and further inland in the poorer parts of Connacht. The CDB itself did not survive the establishment of the Irish Free State in 1922,[1] and the concept of a regional dimension to economic policy in the new state was notable only for its absence from the main economic policies pursued from the 1920s to the early 1950s. When a regional concern re-surfaced in the Underdeveloped Areas Act of 1952, it was again in the context of devising special schemes (grants and subsidies) as incentives to industry to locate in specially designated areas, originally in the western areas of the country. In fact, preferential treatment, in the form of direct subsidies of various kinds, has been since the early 1950s an important aspect of state regional policy for a chain of areas, chiefly along the western seaboard, which are nowadays treated as part of the wider predicament of 'peripheral regions' within the EEC.[2]

However, with the economic growth of the 1960s, concern with the optimum spatial distribution of the benefits of that growth resulted in a re-appraisal of the notion of regional development and regional policy, and in a growing understanding that regional policy meant not only the special problems of the western areas, but rather encompassed an understanding of the implications of all aspects of state policy for the growth and development, relative to each other, of the different regions within the state. Contributing to this new understanding and refinement of the concept of regional policy was the work of a number of research and advisory bodies established in the first flush of enthusiasm for planning and commitment to expertise between 1958 and 1963 *(An Fóras Fórbartha,* whose specific task it was to conduct research and provide the quality advice to the Minister for the Environment for the co-ordination of all aspects of physical planning and growth); the *National Industrial and Economic Council* (later *NESC)* and the *ESRI).* On a practical level an early model of the kind of instrument or agency suitable for regional development was the *Shannon Development Company* (later *SFADCo),* an agency which since its establishment in 1959 has shown unusual initiative in pioneering different aspects of regional development in the mid-western region.[3]

The main landmarks in the development and articulation of a state regional policy during the 1960s and early 1970s can be listed without too much difficulty. [4] Policy developed from the need to think and to plan in spatial terms for two related aspects of the change which occurred during the 1960s and 1970s, physical growth (in its urban and rural forms) and economic growth (employment, incomes and standards of living). The 1963 Local Government (Planning and Development) Act set out clearly the rôle and the powers of the Local Authorities in planned physical growth and also required each Local Planning Authority to draw up development plans at five-yearly intervals. The following year (1964) saw the publication of a report drawn up by the Committee on Development Centres and Industrial Estates. The Report favoured the idea of selecting a number of centres as development centres in a strategy for industrial development. In an analysis of this Report the *National Industrial and Economic Council* in 1965 went even further in stressing the desirability from an economic point of view of concentrating industrial development in a relatively small number of centres or growth-poles, but stated that inadequate infrastructure would rule out wide areas of Connacht and the border counties as suitable locations for such growth centres. Further advice came later in the decade in three special reports from consultants with expertise principally in town planning — Lichfield and Wright, for Limerick and Dublin, respectively, and the Buchanan Report for the rest of the country. The Buchanan Report in particular caused considerable controversy when published in 1968, as it stongly recommended concentration on a small number of growth centres as the most sensible route to industrial development, the strategy strongly favoured by the NIEC. It should be noted that all of these proposals — coming as they did from different groups of experts both within the country and from outside — were contributions to a wider debate which was particularly lively in the 1960s, on the relative advantages of concentration or dispersal of industrial activity as strategies for industrial development. [5] It should also be noted that the view of the Buchanan-NIEC camp, and the advocates of concentration, did not go uncontested. Buchanan's recommended strategy lacked detailed supporting evidence, his Report called for further detailed local studies; and there were reputable economists to be found on both sides of the argument as to whether a growth-centre was the best strategy even in purely economic terms (return on investment in terms of jobs, productivity and profits), leaving aside entirely social and political considerations.

So much for the expert advice being offered during the 1960s. What was the response of the government? What policy was eventually enunciated? Whatever about the particular perspectives which economists or town planners might bring to bear on the question of regional growth, political and social considerations (frequently at an extremely localist level, given the Irish system of political representation and the nature of Irish political culture in general) were bound to loom large in the minds of Irish political leaders. A government statement in 1965 illustrates well the complex set of forces which determined the formulation of regional policy. While accepting that industrial growth centres in areas such as Galway and Waterford would act as a counterbalance to the growth already being experienced in the Limerick-Shannon-Ennis triangle and, especially, in the Dublin region, the government was unwilling to put all its political eggs in such a small number of baskets, and spoke instead of the significant social good which would come of a dispersal of industrial activity. In short, the government did not want to have to choose between high concentration and high dispersal; was anxious to find a golden mean; and held off from any firm commitments pending the completion of the various consultants' reports already commissioned.

By 1969 a comprehensive statement of policy could be deferred no longer. The Buchanan Report demanded a response. Moreover, a large number of development plans had been completed by the local planning authorities (meeting their obligations under the 1963 Act). In retrospect it seems to me that the period between 1968 and 1973 was probably the most fruitful period in the past thirty years for the discussion of regional policy and for some moves towards structural and institutional reforms consistent with the development of a genuine regional policy. A major government statement of May 1969 rejected the model of heavily concentrated industrial development advocated by Buchanan and the NIEC, though it accepted Buchanan's call for more detailed local studies by empowering An Fóras Fórbartha to commission a model development plan for Cork. But the main emphasis of the statement of policy was on the desirability of as wide as possible a dispersal of industrial activity. In particular the policy statement advanced the concept of *regional balance* as the keystone of state regional policy. Specifically it adverted to the disproportionate growth of the Dublin region and its growing dominance within the demographic and economic life of the state; and advocated limiting the further growth of Dublin to the rate of its own natural increase, creating employment in regions other than the eastern region to cater for the natural increase in those regions, and encouraging local authorities to play a dynamic rôle (as 'development corporations') in the retention of population increase through promoting adequate economic growth in the different regions. As for the actual spatial units which were to be designated 'regions', the government in 1969 divided the state into *nine* planning regions, and established Regional Development Organisations (RDOs) to co-ordinate the multiplicity of local development plans (157 in all) and to consolidate them into nine Regional Development Plans. At the same time the IDA was charged with setting up local units and with developing a regional strategy for the creation of industrial employment in conjunction with the RDOs in the nine planning regions. It is worth noting that the experience of SFADCo in the mid-west region (its success in combining industrial promotion activity with a close liaison with officers of local and central government and with voluntary bodies) provided the inspiration for some of the structural reforms introduced in the regional policy initiatives of 1969. The Third Programme for Economic and Social Development, launched in 1969, repeated the newly-stated goals of 'balanced' regional growth, and placed emphasis on the need to facilitate as much as possible the emergence of ideas and initiatives from private and voluntary interests *within* the regions as a key element in regional development (as against the imposition or implantation of ready-made schemes from a central agency). By 1972 the RDOs had completed their regional development plans and the IDA had prepared a series of regional industrial plans, which specified manufacturing employment targets at state, region and town group levels. The IDA strategy was, in their own words, 'neither one of extreme concentration nor extreme dispersal but rather one specially tailored to regional needs and potential'. [6] This was consistent with the major statement of the objectives of state regional policy contained in a government policy statement of May 1972, a statement which drew on both the RDO and the IDA plans. This 1972 statement (probably the most significant statement of regional policy within the past twenty-five years) listed the goals of state regional policy, as being the following:

(i) Assisting the reduction of regional disparities through additional industrial development

(ii) Balanced regional development

(iii) Minimising population dislocation — or involuntary migration — by providing jobs as near as practicable to job seekers

(iv) Restricting industrial development in Dublin to a level consistent with the natural increase in population.

Significantly, while the co-ordinating rôle of the RDOs in preparing the Regional plans was highly praised no executive functions were conferred on them. The county was to remain the basic unit of local government and the county development teams were to play a crucial rôle in encouraging local initiative and enterprise.

It is fair to say that the goals of regional policy declared in 1972 have remained the basic goals of state policy in this area ever since. True, the sectoral emphasis in employment location between regions changed in the light of the impact of the economic difficulties of the 1970s and early 1980s, and in the light of the general shake-out in traditional manufacturing employment under EEC free-trade conditions. Moreover, some commentators have identified in official statements of economic policy in general from the late 1970s an increasing emphasis on self-help or 'bottom-up' community development as a key element in regional renewal and growth. [7] But the *basic* goals of regional policy have not changed since they were first enunciated in the early 1970s. In 1977 the White Paper on National Development spoke of 'the Government's concern that industrial development should provide for an even spread of development throughout the country'. [8]

How successful have we been in meeting these declared goals of regional policy? How have we fared in achieving 'balanced' regional development during the past twenty-five years? Before answering these questions, a word or two about the goals themselves and about the areas specified as planning regions in 1969. There are bound to be difficulties and defects in any scheme which seeks to divide up a state into different regions for planning purposes. On what basis — of geography, population, existing or historical political or administrative units — should the division be made and the boundaries drawn? These are problems which arise in all attempts at regional planning, and in the case of the nine regions into which the state territory was divided, some of these nine regions are more problematic than others (for example, the north-eastern region stretches almost as far west as Loch Erne, and Donegal as a distict planning region suffers from the way in which the border affects its 'natural' geographical orientation towards Derry). However, making due allowance for the difficulties inherent in the regional mapping itself, let us consider what has actually happened in the way of regional balance during the past twenty-five years.

Let us state at once that the declared goals of regional policy have not been achieved. The growth of Dublin has not been checked. In fact the Eastern Region has continued to grow disproportionately throughout this period. That is to say, its *share* of total national population and of total employment has continued to grow, and on present indications this imbalance will become even more exaggerated in the years ahead. The Eastern Region's share of national population has grown from 32% in 1961 to 34% in 1966, to 38% in 1981. Dublin itself has grown to the point where it now accounts for about a third of the national population, an exceptionally high share by northern European standards. [9] This is not to say, of course, that regional employment strategies had no impact at all, or that some of the initiatives in regional development of the past two decades have not been fruitful in different ways. But the central objective of regional policy has not been achieved. In terms of the relationship between the Eastern Region and all other regions in the state the imbalance has become more rather than less pronounced during the past twenty-five years. Why or how did this happen? It is not possible in the space available here to do more than list some of the main factors which may account for our failure to even advance towards the basic objectives of balanced regional development.

Some of the basic assumptions were faulty. For example, given the demographic developments of the 1960s, and the momentum built up in the Dublin region, the objective of merely limiting the growth of Dublin to its natural increase was not calculated to check, still less reverse, the growing dominance of the Eastern Region within the state. Again, the agricultural sector did not make the contribution to regional balance hoped for and expected of it. [10] Continuing employment losses in agriculture throughout the period since 1960 affected other regions more than they affected the Eastern Region. The Common Agricultural Policy of the EEC, in particular the price-support system which favoured certain kinds of production and certain kinds of producers more than others, had the result, when translated into spatial terms in Ireland, of widening still further the gap between the agriculturally more developed and the less developed regions of the country. Special 'packages' of aid for the western and border counties have gone some way towards compensating for the impact of the main CAP policies on regional inequalities. Moreover, recent changes in the CAP itself are likely to have significant implications for inter-regional incomes and output in the agricultural sector in Ireland. But the fact remains that the employment losses in agriculture during the past twenty-five years in the regions outside of Dublin added to the task of finding enough employment outside of agriculture to cater for a growing population and labour force outside of Dublin. Here we come to the heart of the matter. Because if any one factor can be identified as being the key factor in explaining the failure to achieve the goal of 'regional balance' during the past twenty-five years, then it seems to me that this factor was an over-concentration on industrial employment as the over-riding factor in achieving regional balance. In fact, it is scarcely an exaggeration to say that in the years after 1973 the difficult task of formulating a comprehensive and integrated regional policy at state level was virtually abandoned in favour of concentrating on a regional employment strategy in manufacturing employment under IDA auspices. This is not to denigrate the efforts of the IDA to contribute to a better regional balance in industrial development, particularly in the years 1973-79. During these years the national share of manufacturing employment of some of the hitherto weaker regions — the West, and North-West and Midlands — did indeed increase. The Eastern Region's share of total national employment in industrial manufactures fell slightly. The preferential packages of aids and subsidies prepared by the IDA for the weaker regions contributed to this slight shift during the 1970s. So also did the heavy loss of jobs in traditional industries within the Eastern Region in the highly competitive conditions in which Irish industry was now operating. By 1979 the job losses in manufacturing industry in the Eastern Region were so heavy that the IDA had to take corrective action (endorsed by the government) in offering new inducements to industrialists to locate in parts of the Eastern Region badly hit by unemployment in manufacturing. Similar packages have been prepared for other industrial black-spots (such as Cork) in the past five years. [11]

However, even though manufacturing industry suffered in the Eastern Region during the 1970s, this region was the *only* one of the nine planning regions to increase its share of over-all national employment during these years. The reasons for this apparent paradox are not hard to find. Manufacturing employment only accounted for about 20% of total employment in the state by the early 1980s. The obsessive concern of government spokesmen and of many of the general public with IDA figures (often targets) for manufacturing employment, ignored the fact that the greatest growth in employment occurred in the service and other non-manufacturing categories. And throughout the 1970s the Eastern Region — and the Dublin area in particular — increased its share of this service-type employment. [12]

Crucial to this development has been the rôle of public sector employment in our heavily contralised state. As public sector employment grew from the 1960s to the late 1970s — in the central bureaucracy and in state or semi-state agencies — it was heavily centralised in the Eastern Region. This type of employment, as studies have shown, induces further employment. Banking, insurance, information and other services like to be at the centre of the decision-making process. Moreover, the weight of population growth in itself stimulated service employment within the Eastern Region (and to a lesser extent in the main urban centres of the other regions).

The excessive degree of centralisation in Irish government and administration has been remarked on and criticised by a host of distinguished commentators for a considerable time; and at irregular intervals various governments have genuflected in the direction of what they describe as 'decentralisation' schemes. In 1967, for example, the government annouced the 'decentralisation' of two government departments to provincial towns, and twelve years later, in 1979, a White Paper on National Development contained a commitment that 'all new government sector services will be located outside of Dublin unless there are compelling reasons to the contrary', and further promised to tranfer 2,000 civil servants 'to about eight medium sized urban areas in the provinces'. [13] The actual results to-date — which have involved relatively small numbers — have been most disappointing. Of course, this particular brand of decentralisation — what Tom Barrington caustically describes as 'dropping fragments of public bodies in provincial towns'[14] — is, in fact, more correctly a policy of re-location of administrative personnel. The more radical version of decentralisation advocated by Barrington and others involves cutting down 'big', centralised government, and distributing real discretion, and real powers for making and implementing decisions more evenly among communities, through a root and branch reform of the structures of local government. Proposals for sweeping local government changes made in the early 1970s foundered on the rocks of political and bureaucratic conservatism and inertia, and recent reforms in the Dublin region are, in effect, a late respose to the consequences of unregulated growth. [15] In general terms the powers of local authorities relative to central government have diminished during the past fifteen years. Furthermore, a government inter-departmental committee set up in 1975 (on foot of recommendations in the Devlin Report of 1969) to examine how best to co-ordinate the functions of central government and of local authorities at a regional or sub-national level, has not resulted in any action to date.

It would be wrong to suggest that no moves whatever have been made in developing regional structures. The eight regional Health Boards (established under the 1970 Health Act), despite their internal tensions and despite the fact that they are almost totally dependent on the national exchequer for their funds, represent a step along the road of regional planning in a vital area of national infrastructure. Again, in view of the findings of the Clancy Report on the importance of location as a determinant of participation-rates in third-level education, it is worth noting that recent proposals from the Minister for Education suggest that another major area of infrastructure — namely, education — may be the subject of regional planning in the future, though here it is too early to judge the intrinsic merits or the likely outcome of what are as yet but proposals for discussion. [16] One could cite further examples — from the Arts Council to the housing programme — where a regional dimension can be clearly identified.

However, it is the uneven, partial nature of these initiatives, the lack of a coherent and comprehensive strategy, with appropriate institutions and instruments of policy, that is most striking and most depressing. The disappointing levels of relocation and the limited degree of genuine decentralisation during the past twenty years, when public sector employment was growing strongly, has contributed significantly to a momentum of growth in the Eastern Region which will be very difficult to even moderate in the next twenty years, to say nothing of checking or reversing it. The expert opinion available to planners in the Eastern Region itself does not anticipate a check in growth. [17] Moreover, the fact that employment forecasts on a state-wide and sectoral basis suggests a heavy reliance on service-type employment in job-creation in the coming decade or so, make the lost opportunities of the bureaucratic boom years for relocation or genuine decentralisation especially galling, and make the task of achieving an acceptable form of regional balance in the next twenty-five years extremely daunting. [18]

Critics of the excessive centralisation of government, administration and services in Ireland insist that their case rests on more than merely an imbalance in numbers or bulk. There is also an intellectual, psychological and sociological dimension to the problem. The concentration of so large a share of the expertise, the decision-makers, the opinion-shapers into one area is, it is argued, unhealthy on many different grounds: it draws off vital intellectual and other energies from the other regions; encourages a passive or dependency attitude among the 'receivers', in the regions, of decisions made in Dublin; and in a multitude of ways encourages a one-way information and culture flow within the state. It seems to me that a word or two of caution is called for in judging these claims. The fruits of rapid urban growth are not all benign, as the experience of Dublin in recent decades has clearly shown. The heavy concentration of enlightened experts within the Dublin region has not saved that region from some of the common disadvantages or disutilities of rapid urban growth — rising crime levels, vandalism, enclaves of inner city decay, pollution (air and noise), sharp social contrasts and social tension within the metropolitan area. Expert advice — however enlightened — is not always heeded, especially if it is in conflict with powerful forces operating in the market place. In any assessment of regional inequalities or imbalances both sides of the balance sheet of Dublin's rapid growth must be taken into the reckoning.

So far as the dominance of Dublin in the flow of information, ideas, and attitudes is concerned, we may look briefly at the rôle of broadcasting in the cultural flows between regions during the past two decades. [19] In this context the state service (theoretically enjoying a monopoly position within the state) has been disappointing, given the opportunities provided by changing technology, in facilitating genuine culture flows between and within the different regions in the country. Those who find this verdict harsh will probably point to the financial constraints on RTÉ; to the development of Cork local radio, to the experiments in community radio conducted in numerous towns throughout the country in recent years, and to the development of Radio na Gaeltachta to serve the highly dispersed Irish-speaking communities throughout the country. And I would certainly agree that in the matter of 'regional equity' in broadcasting, radio has done considerably better than television. Still, even in radio broadcasting, the limited nature of the experiments in local community radio (and the tardiness which marked their development) has probably contributed to the emergence of the illegal or pirate stations in recent years. In fairness to RTÉ it may be said that the same people (in different governments) who have withheld from RTÉ the funds which might have enabled it to operate a full network of local radio broadcasting, have shown a remarkable tolerance for illegal stations which have sought, in many instances, to substitute for RTÉ as a local or community broadcasting service.

The television service has show less enterprise in trying to achieve 'regional balance' in its output. In this medium the trend of the past twenty-five years has been towards increasing deregulation in the supply of programme material, as more and more areas become (through cable or booster signals) an effective part of a multi-channel television network. In this context RTÉ is often little more than a mediating influence for the more general flow of Anglo-American material which dominates all the networks available in Ireland. The climate is obviously a difficult one for the under-funded national broadcasting service of a small state geographically and culturally situated as we are. But, when all due allowances are made, RTÉ television cannot really be counted among the more outstanding contributors to 'regional balance' in the past twenty-five years.

In this brief essay of the regional dimension of economic and social change in Ireland during the past twenty-five years we have concentrated on those aspects of change where the state has been in a position to exert a significant influence. There are, of course, many aspects of our economic development where external forces, often largely immune to interference or regulation at the level of national government, can impinge powerfully on the pattern of regional development. We in Ireland have become familiar with these facts in the past twenty five years, chiefly as a result of our experience of large transnational companies. In this context of the impact of powerful external and market forces, it is worth reminding ourselves that at the time of our accession to the EEC it was confidently forecast that our membership would enable us to benefit from considerable transfers as part of a specific EEC commitment to reduce inter-regional inequalities within the Community. A key instrument for effecting these particular kinds of inter-regional transfers and for regional development in general was to have been the Regional Fund of the Community. The impact of this Regional Fund in reducing inter-regional inequalities has been disappointing to date from an Irish point of view (though many different projects in Ireland have been helped from the Fund). Part of this disappointment is due to the failure at Community level to formulate an adequate Regional Policy for the Community as a whole. But our own failure to develop a comprehensive and coherent regional policy at national level has not helped us in making the best use of what is available to us under the Regional Fund even as it stands. The accession of the Mediterranean states to the EEC has already given a new impetus to the debate on inter-regional transfers and on regional policy in general. We in Ireland should welcome the re-opening of this debate. Instead of seeing these new Mediterranean members of the EEC as competitors for the scarce surpluses provided for peripheral regions by the wealthier states of the EEC, we should see them rather as potential allies in pressing for a major effort to effect real transfers on an inter-regional basis within the EEC. This may call for a thorough re-assessment of our position within the EEC.

However, if we are to play any significant part in the re-formulation of EEC regional policy we will have to show more political skill and sophistication, more ideas and energy in carrying out major reforms in our own structures of government and administration at a national and sub-national level within Ireland, than we have shown during the past twenty-five years. The task of achieving an acceptable form of regional balance in economic and social development within the state is more difficult today than it was a quarter century ago. On the evidence of the past twenty-five years it is difficult to be optimistic about our prospects of checking the growth of the Eastern Region and securing a better regional balance, while present structures of government and administration obtain, and while we continue to lack a comprehensive and integrated state regional policy.

13. The Church and Change

Desmond Fisher

Psychologists tell us that people generally do not like change. Anything that threatens our convictions or seriously upsets our patterns of behaviour is unwelcome.

We seem most averse to change in matters of religion. We resent having to alter our habits of religious practice or to modify deeply-held religious beliefs. Perhaps this is because our formal religious education usually ends when we leave school where we have learned by conditioning, not through personal understanding and commitment.

Yet the philosophers' teaching and experience confirm that change is part of the human condition. Human organisms change all the time. And since the Church is composed of human beings, the logic is that it must constantly change too.

Few Irish Catholics would have argued in this vein — in public at least — twenty-five years ago. Any of us over say thirty years of age will remember the way we were taught our religion. We were indoctrinated with the belief — however historically inaccurate — that the Roman Catholic Church does not alter. We were presented with the image of the Church as rock-firm, unchanging. We were expected to look to it for certainties, for detailed rules of behaviour, for the answers to all of life's problems.

It was just at the beginning of the twenty-five-year time-span which this series of Thomas Davis Lectures is examining that a very changed vision of the Church began to be propounded. A few years later, this vision was to be incorporated into the teaching of an Ecumenical Council, the most authoritative teaching body in the Catholic Church.

The Second Vatican Council was summoned by Pope John XXIII and was held from 1962 to 1965. John's motive in summoning it was to 'update' the Church, to present it in a new way to the world. To do that, he recognised that the Church would have not only to speak to the world but also to listen to it. It had to interpret what he called 'the signs of the times', that is, the new insights the world had developed. The Church, he felt, must change — not its basic doctrines but the way it understood them and presented them to the world.

Of the sixteen Constitutions, decrees and declarations it promulgated, the Council's Dogmatic Constitution on the Church was the most important. The image it presented of the Church was very different from the one which was being proferred to Irish Catholics twenty-five years ago.

The Council saw the Church as a fellowship, an assembly of the people of God. It saw its members on a pilgrim journey through life. Each one of us — Pope, prelate, priest, parishioner — has a mission, a vocation. That vocation is to change ourselves and by so doing to change the people around us so that eventually the whole world is changed into what God wants it to be, into His kingdom.

The idea of change is intrinsic to this understanding of what the Church is. The Council saw our membership of the Church — our religion — as the motivating force for producing the right change in the world around us.

To a person of my age, it is a sobering thought that the Second Vatican Council which was the most important event in my forty years of journalism, is outside the personal experience of anyone in this country under thirty years of age or so. And that, according to the sociologists, is a third of the people of Ireland.

These people do not know what life was like in Catholic Ireland before the Council. They have not experienced the narrowness of attitude in which people of my generation were reared. They are probably unaware that Catholics were forbidden to attend Protestant weddings and funerals. They have not to weigh ounces of bread to ensure that the fasting regulations are obeyed. Their religious formation is not, like ours was, determined, in part at least, by the external pressure to conform — certainly to nothing like the same extent. Hell-fire has fewer terrors now. Love, not fear, is taught as the motivating force of Christianity.

Young people in Ireland today do not appreciate, therefore, the changes which the Second Vatican Council helped bring about in this country — the liturgical innovations, the ecumenical advances, the removal of the overwhelming sense of life as a sort of examination process in which the course itself did not matter but only the passing of the final judgement.

Today's youth has no reference point, no model of yesterday's 'before' to contrast with today's 'after'. Two decades after the end of the Council, however, the changes have been considerable. Irish Catholics in general are no longer as willing to spurn material comforts in this life to ensure a higher reward in the life to come. Relative affluence is morally acceptable and higher living standards regarded as a right. Dogmatism is questioned, as better education and foreign travel create a greater openness to new ideas and value systems. Clerical paternalism and authoritarianism are resented and there is a changed attitude to moral questions. Women call for change in a church which they feel treats them as second-class citizens. A more tolerant attitude, the result in part of reaction to the Northern Ireland 'troubles', challenges the view that Catholicism is uniquely and exclusively true.

Adding to the impetus of all these influences, there has been an immense growth in the volume and immediacy of communications. Television in particular is disseminating attitudes and values which otherwise would not be so pervasive and so persuasive.

Suddenly, it seems, Ireland has been immersed in a ferment of influences and stimuli which other countries have had a much longer time to assimilate. Each of these influences has had a different effect in Ireland. Individually, their impact may have been limited and uneven; collectively they have combined to challenge traditionally accepted religious attitudes and behaviour.

Some Catholics have found the new climate stimulating· and liberating. They have accepted the changes in both secular and religious thought as 'signs of the times', that is, as necessary to greater understanding of the way the Christian faith should be lived in today's world. They are no longer satisfied with the old formulations and formulae. They disagree in public with the way that Catholic teaching is expressed or, more frequently, reject it in private. Some, especially the young, have given up religious practice, perhaps even religious belief, altogether. On the other hand there are those Catholics who are unhappy with what they see as a betrayal of the true faith and an abandonment of its basic teachings. They feel that those advocating change are not genuinely committed Christians. They see any updating, as Pope John XXIII called the Second Vatican Council process, as a dangerous dilution of the Church's doctrine. Pluralism they regard as a surrender to religious indifferentism and unbelief.

The depth of the divide between the two approaches has surfaced most clearly in the interface between religion and politics, especially in the context of the controversies over the Constitutional Referendum on abortion and over legislation on contraception and divorce. The bitterness of the controversies, notably the campaigns waged by lay organisations on both sides of the debate, shows that the uniformity — or was it just conformity? — which used to be the dominant characteristic of Irish Catholicism is no more. Its distinguishing mark now, at least on the level of public debate, is its divisiveness. Cardinal Ó Fiaich's judgement, in his statement at the beginning of the Extraordinary Synod of Bishops last November, that polarisation has been avoided in the Irish Catholic Church would not be accepted by everyone.

Polarisation may, indeed, be hurtful and alarming to people who measure the health of the Church by the degree of uniformity in its practice. Others see it as a sign of growth, a recognition that Catholics can agree on essentials while disagreeing on matters not central to the faith.

The difference between the two 'wings' of the Church is obscured by the high, though declining, level of religious practice in Ireland. The statistics of attendance at weekly Mass, at the 'Easter duties' and similar exercises where participation can be measured quantitatively, are impressive. If external behaviour were the test of a people's faith, Ireland would head all the league tables.

What cannot be measured, however, is what some writers have called the 'internal migration' from the Church. This is the alienation experienced by some Catholics — no one can put a number to them — who feel that the Church is not relevant to today's needs and who regard religious practice as a duty which custom, social conformity or the fear of Hell-fire impose on them. They find it difficult to pray. Sermons bore them. They feel no sense of participation or of an experience of community in the sacraments.

Catholics who feel like this do not — even if they could — force their reluctant children to attend religious services. They are not themselves so convinced of the genuineness of the religious experience they encounter to impose it on anyone else.

What, then will happen to the statistics of religious practices when the next generation and the one after that come to maturity? A continuation of the present trend could, by the end of the century, halve the current attendance figures. The Catholic Church in Ireland faces the possibility of becoming a minority Church, minority in the sense that most of those nominally subscribing to it would not be practising to the minimum extent prescribed by the rules.

Catholic theologians like Karl Rahner and Edward Schillebeeckx have predicted that the Catholic Church in general faces a new *diaspora*. By that they mean that Catholicism will be practised by an ever-declining number of adherents who will have to form small catacomb-like communities to retain their identities.

Ireland may be the last country for which such a future could be contemplated. But the experience of Spain and France — not to mention Italy — shows that, once the decline in religious practice sets in, it develops rapidly. There can be no guarantee that Ireland will escape a similar process.

It is understandable that the bishops, seeing the decline in religious practice, should judge it to be the result of a decline in the faith itself and should see the remedy in a crusade to restore the faith to its former vitality. This was surely the motivation for the hierarchy's invitation to the Pope to visit Ireland in 1979.

What this approach ignores is that faith works in and through a particular culture. It finds a specific expression in that culture at a particular time. The result is a nexus of religious attitudes, practices and understandings — in short, a particular theology — which is part and parcel of that culture. If the culture changes, the theology which is part of it will change too, though the basic faith from which the theology sprang remains the same. Crusades to prevent the theology from changing in the wake of cultural change or to restore it to what it was before a cultural change will inevitably fail.

The mistake which the Irish bishops may be making is to regard theology like the basics of the faith itself as uniform and immutable. The fundamental lesson of the Second Vatican Council was that this is not so. The Council showed that unity does not demand uniformity, that theology can change, that different theologies can flourish at the same time, though the underlying faith is unaffected.

All the world over, cultures are changing and theologies with them. There is now a black theology in South Africa and other countries; a liberation theology in Latin America; a feminist theology in the United States. Theology is no longer seen to be unitary, universal, uniform, but many-stranded, localised and pluriform.

A country which tolerates a variety of cultural influences can accept or reject new ideas with no great public upset. One with a more rigid and cohesive cultural ethos, in which social attitudes and religious values cross-validate each other or are made to conform, at least superficially, by an authoritarian clerical establishment can resist new influences only as long as each one of the pillars on which its culture rests remains firm. Once a single support is weakened, the whole structure is in danger of collapse.

Something like this is what has been happening in Ireland. The nexus between language, religion, nationalism, social behaviour has begun to come apart. First, the language was lost. Then, with the winning of Independence for part of the country, the forces of nationalism were largely spent. More recently, better education, the communications explosion, affluence, foreign travel, the stress on personal freedoms and the rest of the influences noted earlier have changed cultural patterns and, consequently, religious attitudes. As the cultural ethos changes, the real or imposed socio-religious integration dissolves.

It is impossible for Church leaders, if that is what they seek, to restore traditional patterns of religious behaviour and outlook which developed from a now-discarded cultural ethos. The old culture is dead and with it the old theology. The only way to re-integrate religion with ordinary life — which is what Christians are called on to do — is to develop a new theology to meet the needs of the times.

Karl Rahner, the German Jesuit theologian, said what the world needs today is:

a theology of the mysteries of Christ, of the physical world, of time and temporal relations, of history, of sin, of man, of birth, of eating and drinking, of work, of seeing, hearing, talking, weeping, laughing, of music, of dance, of culture, of television, of marriage and the family, of ethnic groups and the state of humanity.

Or, as Yves Congar, the French Dominican, put it more succinctly, we have to provide 'a contemporary church in a contemporary world'.

The Irish bishops did not distinguish themselves at the Vatican Council. Like most of the bishops from the English-speaking world, they had come to Rome unacquainted with the work of the Continental European theologians who had laid most of the foundations for the eventual Council pronouncements. And unlike their colleagues in Britain, North America, Australia and parts of Africa, they did not share the conversion from conservatism to what could be described as middle-of-the-road open-mindedness which was the general experience.

The reaction of most of the Irish bishops fell somewhere between the positions adopted respectively by Archbishop McQuaid of Dublin and Cardinal Conway of Armagh. For Dr McQuaid, 'nothing had happened in Rome to disturb the tranquillity of Irish Catholic life'. For him, apparently, the Second Vatican Council might never have been.

Cardinal Conway was shrewder. He saw that changes would inevitably come. He determined that they would come in a way and at the speed which the official Church wanted. The people would be told what the changes would be, how they would be introduced and, in any case, as was drummed out from every pulpit, they were not really changes at all but reversions to an older ecclesiastical practice.

Undoubtedly, there was a need both to reassure those Catholics, mainly the older ones, who resented change of any kind that the essence of the faith remained intact and to restrain those who would take reform to excess. But the whole thrust of Cardinal Conway's campaign — for it could be called that — was to capture and control the forces of change so that they could be packaged and rationed out as the bishops determined.

Of the two approaches, that of Archbishop McQuaid, though felt at the time to be almost a repudiation of the Council, was probably the less harmful. He proved to be — in this context at least — an ecclesiastical Canute, powerless to stop the tide of the Council.

What Cardinal Conway did was arguably more prejudicial. The thrust of the Council's work was to present a new vision of the Church as the people of God, to establish the centrality of the laity's vocation and to see change — which was called *aggiornamento* or 'updating' — as essential to the fulfilment of the Church's rôle and mission.

The Cardinal's approach, however, was to keep control in the hands of the institutional Church and measure out the liturgical and other changes in small doses that could be absorbed without what he considered as dangerous. The result was that the old rules were replaced by new rules, better rules certainly, but still externally-imposed rules. Irish Catholics were thus deprived of much of the impetus for change and for personal involvement in determining that change which the Council intended to impart.

In particular, the Catholic Church in Ireland was denied the new understanding of the role of the laity which was one of the most important contributions of the Council. Before the Second Vatican Council, a lay person was seen in theology in negative terms. A lay person was a non-cleric, a passive participant whose rôle, as one bishop said sarcastically at the Council, was seen as to believe, to pray, to obey and to pay. The Council expressed a far nobler vision:

> By reason of their special vocation (it said), it belongs to the laity to seek the kingdom of God by engaging in temporal affairs and directing them according to God's will. They live in the world, that is, they are engaged in each and every work and business of the earth and in the ordinary circumstances of social and family life which, as it were, constitute their very existence. There they are called by God that, being led by the spirit of the Gospel, they may contribute to the sanctification of the world, as from within like a leaven, by fulfilling their own particular duties.[1]

This is a very different sort of thinking from the emphasis on devotionalism, conformity and meek acceptance of clerical authoritarianism which has been the tradition in Ireland and is still prevalent in many parts of the country. In another document, the Council instructed pastors 'to be sincere in their appreciation and promotion of lay people's dignity and of the special rôle the laity have to play in the Church's mission'.[2]

Giving lay people duties like reading the lessons, distributing Communion and collecting money is not what the Council was talking about. These are quasi-clerical duties. Appointing selected — not elected — lay people to parish councils and episcopal committees still avoids the real issue.

The rôle of the lay person, as the Council saw it, is to be more than a second-class cleric. The model of the lay person's holiness as presented by the Council is not a watered-down version of that of the priest or nun. The lay person is seen as achieving holiness in doing the ordinary work of the world in a special way.

If one is to judge by the reports of his contributions to the recent Extraordinary Synod of Bishops, Cardinal Ó Fiaich is closer to the spirit of the Council than his predecessor in Armagh and, indeed, than most of his contemporaries in the present hierarchy.

Some priests and religious are also far in advance of the general body of the Church in their understanding of the Second Vatican Council. Nuns especially have gone through a renewal process which has been far more thorough and rejuvenating than anything achieved by most people in the other parts of the Church. Younger priests, like those in the National Conference of Priests, are developing insights, derived from the Council, into the meaning of ministry, which could, if accepted generally, transform their relationship with the laity. Small lay groups are meeting to study the Scriptures, to discuss current issues in the light of the Gospel and of Conciliar teaching and generally to develop an adult spirituality.

The future of the Catholic Church in Ireland depends on whether these and other initiatives can produce a new theology before the traditional moulds of Irish Catholicism shatter under the pressure of cultural change. To attempt to force it into a return to the old dogmatic certainties, the rules and regulations of the pre-Conciliar age, is a counsel of despair.

A programme for the post-Conciliar Catholic Church in Ireland would involve a new understanding of holiness as consisting not of spurning and avoiding the world but as working whole-heartedly within it to change it. It would encourage personal responsibility — in the family, in the workplace, in society as a whole — instead of an escapist devotionalism and emotionalism. It would teach Christianity as a positve commitment to Christ-like values rather than negatively as minimalist avoidance of breaches of detailed Mosaic precepts. It would end clerical dogmatism and authoritarianism, seeing Christianity as a constant and continuing search for truth rather than as obedience to a Truth already established in all its dimensions for all time.

It would recognise that the separate rôles of all parts of the Church — Pope, bishops, priests, nuns, laymen and, perhaps particularly, laywomen — are essential to the good of the whole and would ensure that each section is allowed to function fully as it is intended to.

It would also — and this is particularly relevant — find a way for the bishops to fulfil their responsibilities as pastors without impinging on the different rôle of legislators — a point well made by Dr Cahal Daly in his New Year address on the Northern Ireland scene.

The challenge to the Catholic Church in Ireland — and, indeed, to the Christian churches everywhere — is to develop a theology to meet the needs of our times. It has to adapt or die. Given our belief

in the Church's indefectibility — that it will never fail — we must
expect it to change, require it to change, help it to change.

As the inevitable Latin tag has it, *Ecclesia semper reformanda* —
the Church must always be in the process of being reformed. Church
and change are inseparable.

14. Politics and Change

Brian Farrell

The creation of The Economic and Social Research Institute twenty-five years ago was at once a symbol and a symptom of change in Irish life. This series of Thomas Davis Lectures to mark the anniversary of its foundation has documented and analysed the major strands of those changes. Since Independence, Ireland had exhibited many characteristics of a post-colonial, less developed country: a low standard of living, high dependence on primary agricultural production for jobs and exports, excessive emigration and high unemployment. From the late 1950s an economic transformation began which — viewed from the perspective of the 1980s — seems almost a golden age of growth. It was accompanied by changes in the size, structure and spread of population that reversed trends which had persisted in Ireland for more than a century. The combination of rapid economic change with a demographic revolution was accompanied by a fundamental shift in the technology of communication. Inevitably, as the society moved, so did its social institutions, concerns and rhetoric — and at least some of its social attitudes, as Finola Kennedy has discussed in an earlier essay.

How did all of this affect Irish political life? In politics, too, there were visible, tangible changes. The founding-fathers, who had worked to create the Irish state and divided on the issue of the Treaty debate had dominated leadership in parliament, government and parties for nearly forty years. The election of De Valera as president of Ireland in 1959 marked the effective eclipse of that generation.

Although Seán Lemass had belonged and contributed to its power, he was identified with the new wave of economic growth, social change and administrative innovation. [1] No rhetorician, he encapsulated the unreflective optimism of the new Ireland with the belief that a rising tide lifts all boats: that view has been critically analysed by Peter Cassells in this book.

Irish political discourse, so long focused on a narrow band of essentially rhetorical themes relating to sovereignty, constitutional relations with Britain, the re-unification of the national territory and the restoration of the Irish language, changed in tone, content and emphasis. Bread-and-butter issues of employment, inflation and taxation had always been part of political debate and electoral campaigning. But they had been peripheral to a basic partisan cleavage that owed more to the accidents of history and personality than to social class or economic self-interest. Despite the efforts of the Labour Party, inherited loyalties rather than ideological debate had determined partisan preference for the vast majority of voters. The major parties had avoided ideological labels.

Although questions of economic management now began to provide the central agenda for Irish political discourse, they appear to have had little effect on major party policy. The two main parties have continued to compete for a large, agreed middle ground of the electorate and have been reluctant to clarify policy differences. Fianna Fáil and Fine Gael over the last quarter-century have shared a common view that favours a pragmatic, mixed economy response to the agreed evils of high unemployment and inflation. Typically, when faced with the major issue of membership of the European Communities they closed ranks to present the same set of arguments in favour of entry. While there was some divergence on points of detail in the course of electoral campaigns, there was a fundamental convergence — reflected in Michael Gallagher's comment that the change in the language of Irish politics in the 1960s and 1970s 'signified only that politicians were using different straw from which to make the bricks they hurled at each other, rather than that Irish parties had developed fundamentally different attitudes to subjects around which many west European party systems had traditionally revolved'. [2] Despite three general elections in rapid succession in 1981-82 a broad economic consensus between the major parties has continued to be more important than any clear policy difference between them.

The eruption of conflict in Northern Ireland might have provided another possible source of ideological distinction between the parties. It could have revived the embers of old civil war divisions; it did raise the cluster of knotty questions about relations with Britain and the northern communities, about law and order, subversion and political censorship. It did intensify existing factional strains within Fianna Fáil. [3] But from the Arms Crisis through Sunningdale and a series of Anglo-Irish summits to the New Ireland Forum and Hillsborough, disagreements between parties about the Republic's attitude towards the north have been tonal, stylistic and marginal rather than substantive. Irrespective of which group was in power, the opposition has been prepared to score debating points and offer criticism. But both sides of the partisan domestic competition have shared an approach in government marked by moderation, pragmatism, incrementalism and an agreed analysis of the nature of the Northern Ireland problem. [4] The north has sometimes been allowed to become a football in the games political parties play; it is not a definitive way of distinguishing between the teams. 'The Northern conflict' in Terence Brown's phrase, 'did not stimulate major ideological redirection in the Republic'. [5]

The northern dimension has been part of the wider discussion of social questions in Irish politics in the last twenty-five years. Population changes, industrialisation, urbanisation, communication, the emergence of the women's movement have all contributed to an expanded political agenda. In the context of a society that was so stable that it could be regarded as stagnant for forty years, many of the topics raised were contentious. The rôle of the Roman Catholic Church — its hierarchy, institutions and authority — began to be explored, as Desmond Fisher has discussed in his essay. Taboo subjects of contraception, divorce and abortion were catapulted into prominence. However, it is noticeable that the politicians were more prone to respond to, rather than initiate, the public debate on such issues. Increasingly, it was small, energetic and unrepresentative voluntary groups that forced the pace of change. Although some argue that 'Fianna Fáil has placed itself firmly on the "right" of the political spectrum' in a range of such issues, it is clear that Dr FitzGerald's constitutional crusade has failed to overcome resistance and inertia within his own party. [6] On social issues, as on economic management and Northern Ireland, the major political parties prefer to express the difference between them in general terms of competence, credibility and personality rather than in the sharper terms of ideological choice.

The continuing conservative character of party politics is revealed in the composition of successive Dála. The electorate was changing — population growth, economic advance, increased urbanisation, enhanced education ensured that. The most recent comprehensive study of Dáil deputies in the 1980s shows that:

while the age levels, educational and occupational backgrounds of Dáil deputies have followed definite trends towards the norm for countries at more advanced stages of development, this does not appear to have made any impression on the routes this changing breed of prospective politicians take to the Dáil. [7]

Family connection and sporting prowess underline the continuing emphasis on localism and personalism in Irish parliamentary representation. Whether considered as the result of the spread of a friend's and neighbour's relationship from rural into urban Ireland, as the outcome of severe administrative failure to deal with public needs and wants, or as a direct effect of the competition induced by the electoral system, the rôle of the deputy has remained extraordinary limited. [8] Typically deputies have ignored their legislative functions and concentrated on a parochial level of representation. To date, there is little evidence that attempts to reform the procedures of the Dáil — a persistent if minor theme in political discussion through the 1970s beginning to be implemented in the 1980s — have significantly increased the rôle of deputies in policy formulation, financial control or effective scrutiny of government.

These elements of structural stability seem to contradict a common impression that the 1970s and 1980s have marked a period of change and upheaval in Irish politics. There has been considerable discussion of the volatility of recent elections, implying more violent swings in party support than have occurred in the past. Some such oscillation of political opinion and behaviour might have been expected in the light of the extensive social and economic changes of the period. It seems confirmed in the fact that every general election since 1969 has resulted in an alternation of parties in government. However, these relatively rapid changes in government — although they may have contributed to a sense of uncertainty or instability — had more to do with the way a sophisticated electoral system produces accurate proportional representation than with any sudden swings in partisan support.

Certainly, there have been significant changes in party support in recent elections. It is possible to examine them most closely in the results of the three most recent elections, fought in the same constituencies within a very short time period. Those contests also provide an opportunity to test whether the description of 'politics without social bases' still applies; with major changes in society is it possible to discern in contemporary politics a relationship between social class and partisan preference conspicuously lacking in an earlier period? [9]

The most intensive analysis of these results by Richard Sinnott indicates that the traditional picture has not, as yet, been significantly altered. Fianna Fáil support had a slightly less cross-class character. Fine Gael 'edged towards becoming the party of the middle-class', although consolidating support among the skilled working-class. Labour, despite the intervention of the Workers' Party, maintained its share of the working class vote, and, in Sinnott's words, 'it would be premature to predict its displacement as the third largest party in the state'. [10] These findings support the conclusion of a wider scrutiny of electoral volatility in the period 1948 - 1983 showing that 'at five of the six elections between 1948 and 1965 net volatility was higher than at any of the six subsequent elections'. [11]

In a situation where the major parties decline to analyse, clarify and articulate the differences between them in terms other than personality and competence, where three parties have successfully captured some 90% of first preference votes, and where candidate-selection is largely related to intensely local and personalistic criteria, the Irish electorate has responded by maintaining a pattern of politics without social bases. Whether the continued efforts of the Workers' Party or the new emergence of the Progressive Democrats can contribute to breaking that established mould remains as yet to be tested. For the moment it seems wise to anticipate that such developments are unlikely to upset the judgement that 'the "end of ideology" dawned in Ireland before ideology had even arrived'. [12]

To date, the Irish party system has been able to cope with, absorb, accommodate, widespread social change without seriously adapting its own basic structure. In response to the communication revolution, the parties have become more professional in their approach to marketing their electoral goods. [13] In response to the women's movement there has been some effort to recruit, nominate and promote women within the parties. In response to a younger population the major parties have created youth sections, employed youth officers and aimed some of their publicity at the younger end of the political market. In response to some evidence of a decline in the authority of organised religion, there have been some attempts to secularise the law and constitution. Yet these moves towards adaptation have been marginal; the parties typically have reacted to, rather than led, public opinion.

That excess of prudence by the major parties — itself a product of their appreciation of a deep conservatism in Irish society — has affected the operation of government. In democratic theory citizens are assumed to register rational choices between programmes offered by competing parties; elections translate these choices into a parliamentary representation which determines the government, assists it in framing the laws required to execute the will of the people and monitors and controls its operations. In reality, parliamentary activity often appears irrelevant. Out-moded procedures prevent the Dáil from debating issues that are the stuff of immediate communcation in the media. Interest groups have by-passed parliament and applied pressure directly on those in government and in administration. Even more important, a new set of structures — formal and informal — have developed in which discussion of and decisions regarding public policy take place.

Earlier in this book Brendan Walsh documented the growth, and cost, of state intervention in the last twenty-five years. He noted that the proliferation of new state agencies was 'the most colourful manifestation of the growth of the public sector'. Some of those agencies also represented an important strategic shift within the governmental structure. The growth of government has been accompanied by what can be described as a new corporatism, the development of institutions and practices through which ministers, civil servants and representatives of the great vocational and sectional interests decide policy and conduct administration. The process is not peculiar to Ireland but it could be argued that the context of the Irish political system has done much to elevate the power of the social partners at the expense of the parties.

The acceptance of planning began, in Professor Joe Lee's phrase, 'a subtle shift in the nature of public decision-making ... Ireland began to shuffle towards a version of the corporate state.' [14] What began as advisory bodies — in particular, the National Industrial Economic Council and its enlarged successor, the National Economic and Social Council — may have been designed to secure the co-operation and involvement of the social partners. They have, in effect, become an alternative to parliament as an arena for public policy-making.

That process accelerated as the small open Irish economy was buffeted by uncontrollable, external forces. The oil crises of 1973 and 1979 plunged the world economy into depression and disaster, to borrow a phrase from Dr Whitaker's essay in this book. The chronic recession then induced, coupled with the tensions of a post-industrial age, have created challenges for employment far outside the shores of these islands. The sense of difficulties wholly or largely outside our control may have encouraged political leaders and their advisers to seek new methods of creating and sustaining some wide-based consensus. But there are clear dangers in developments that give special access and influence to interest groups. Legitimising their role has encouraged a feudal tendency for powerful interest groups to challenge and reject openly the legal decisions of government and parliament. Far from inducing some sense of common purpose, the new corporatism has encouraged the pursuit of narrow self-interest; agencies created to stimulate the economy or tackle particular social issues have become vested interests pursuing their own organisational goals. All of this has contributed to what Tom Barrington has called 'the hastening drift to ungovernability'. [15]

Again, it is not a problem peculiar to Ireland. In other democracies, too, the expansion of state intervention has led to a governmental overload that threatens to overwhelm established political institutions; other parliaments have their authority challenged and their functions questioned; other party systems appear to concentrate on sham battles that are irrelevant to their societies; in other jurisdictions the operation of law and administration has taken on an arcane life, alien to the life of the community it is supposed to serve. The symptoms of popular alienation, centralised corporatism and constipated administration are well-documented. In the Irish case three contributing factors have exacerbated the situation.

One has been the persistence of the northern conflict. The New Ireland Forum estimated the costs of violence arising from the Northern Ireland crisis since 1969. [16] It is impossible to calculate the destabilising effects of an issue which, while ranked low in the electorate's perception of priorities, have absorbed so much governmental time and energy. [17] A second factor has been the impact of a demographic revolution. The third has been the unwillingness of those responsible to recognise the symptoms of ungovernability, let alone confront them.

The major parties have shown little willingness, or even capacity, to adapt themselves to social change. The parliament has been content to remain tied to a parish-pump model of politics irrelevant to its national constituency and has allowed an undefined and unauthorised corporatism to usurp its decision-making functions. Successive governments have been prepared to preside over a slide in the competence of the state to manage its affairs with, as Basil Chubb has noted, 'public expenditure and public sector wage costs out-stripping available resources and with clear signs of over-complex, over-strained political and administrative organisations failing to administer or enforce the law in some areas'. [18]

It says much for the stability of the Irish poltical system and the durability of its institutions that these failures have not, as yet, raised more serious doubts. The experience of three general elections in rapid succession in the early 1980s shattered the cosy conventions of earlier times. The contests gave no simple answer to the question: who forms government? The responses and reactions of politicians to those events breached hitherto accepted standards of behaviour. Close election results and the presence of minor groupings in the Dáil encouraged a tendency to seek power on the basis of political deals rather than a popular mandate. Rivalries within and between parties revolutionised the earlier, relaxed, slow-moving mode of government and ministerial replacement. [19] In the three years from Charles Haughey's first government in 1979 to Garret FitzGerald's second coalition in 1982 a total of twenty-six new cabinet ministers were appointed, compared to only thirty ministers in the first quarter century of the state's existence. While the criteria for ministerial selection and deployment have yet to be analysed it is clear that parliamentary seniority, geographical location in relation to party electoral advantage and personal loyalty to the leader are more significant than questions of capacity and competence. Inevitably, this, added to other developments, elevated the rôle of Taoiseach and encouraged a continuing emphasis on personalism even at the highest level of the Irish political system.

Yet it is evident that much of the — often frenetic — political activity of recent years is largely irrelevant to the basic challenges facing Irish democracy in these later years of the twentieth century. Twenty-five years ago, after a period of decline, if not decay, a small group of political and administrative leaders embarked on a programme of structural reform and policy innovation. Now it is clear that those political ideas and ideals have run their course; the political system and the administrative engine are out of gear within the changing needs of the economy and society.

More is at stake than questions of the competence of governments or the effectiveness of their policies. There are fundamental questions about the legitimacy of government and the capacity of the political system to ensure consent and compliance. The representative system inherited at the foundation of the state has served us well but now the need for adaptation is urgent. The record of efforts to reform the public service and to reform parliament to date may not encourage any great optimism. Even where problems have been analysed and solutions devised there have been distinct failures to implement reform effectively. The way in which proposals for local government reform 'foundered on the rocks of political and bureaucratic conservatism and inertia' have been detailed by Gearóid Ó Tuathaigh in an earlier essay.

If those directly involved in the political process are unwilling to make the effort to change, how can any larger popular consensus be created? The inherent contradiction of attempting to maintain a democratic facade while governing without consensus is all too clearly exemplified by the experience of Northern Ireland. The task of political leadership in the Republic in the 1980s must rise beyond the admittedly daunting tasks of crisis management, go beyond the demanding effort to keep the governmental engine ticking over, rise above the political calculation of merely husbanding support for the next election. It may well be that, in Franklin Roosevelt's phrase, the first duty of the democratic politician is to get elected. That is a necessary, but not a sufficient condition for maintaining the health of a democratic system. The politicians must also see to it that the institutions of government, the policies that direct it and the parties that give it vitality are appropriate to the time, place and circumstance in which they operate. Any consideration of politics and change in Ireland over the last twenty-five years must conclude that precisely those central questions of public philosophy have been progressively evaded. There has been far too little attempt to initiate a new debate about basic principles and objectives, let alone efforts to create a machinery more appropriate to their realisation. That is the task of political leadership in the 1980s. It is a challenge for old and new parties alike.

15. Whither Ireland?
The Next Twenty-Five Years!

Joseph Lee

Prediction is a perilous enterprise. The historian, of all people, must remain acutely aware of the innumerable occasions on which the plot of the human drama has taken unexpected turns. Indeed, a historical perspective counsels against the presumption of the puny human mind, however reinforced by modern technology, in venturing to forecast the future. Futurology has helped sharpen our perspectives on possible future scenarios, but it cannot predict events, however much it may alert us to probable processes. Even the ablest of our economic forecasters notoriously experience great difficulty in predicting quite short-term developments. As late as the summer of 1985, for instance, the Department of Finance, the Central Bank, and OECD and even the ESRI expected a growth of more than 2% in gross domestic product for 1985. It now transpires that the actual growth, if there was any growth at all, was less than 1%. If that can happen in a relatively quantifiable area like economics, and over very short time spans, when it may be assumed that the relevant variables can be reasonably foreseen, the scholar striving to incorporate not only economic trends, but more elusive qualitive factors like intelligence, morality and character into his futuristic scenario has to be only too conscious of the pitfalls. [1] All I shall try to do here is to identify some underlying trends contributing to our present condition, and hazard some suggestions about ways in which we may improve our national performance over the next quarter century.

Our present plight is reflected most vividly in high unemployment, high taxation and high debt. The irresponsible decision taken by the government in 1972 to borrow for day-to-day expenditure has resulted in a spiralling national indebtedness, not least to foreigners. We borrowed mainly to live beyond our means. We were too clever by half. We took our winnings and ran. Now the running, for most of us, has had to stop. Of course there is no perfect justice in the play. Some of the guilty may be able to shift the burden on to the shoulders of the innocent. But the guilty did not take sufficient precaution to ensure that there would be enough innocents to go around. If it is the poorer classes who suffer most hideously from an unemployment level more than double the OECD average, even the more secure classes now find that their children are already beginning to pay the price for the collective greed of the parents. How many reasonably comfortable parents even five years ago confidently expected their children to proceed to third-level education more or less as a matter of course — and now find they cannot afford it after the punitive corrective measures that have had to be imposed to help pay the massive interest on the unproductive debt and to sustain welfare payments at a time of soaring unemployment? Broadening the tax base would help, but not nearly enough, and could in no way compensate for the instability of character that lies at the root of our current problems. The bird that has come home to roost is the albatross.

How then can we plot an escape route from the morass? We must begin by developing a capacity for strategic thinking. By strategic thinking I mean thinking about the direction of national development over the next five to twenty-five years, thinking about how we want the country to develop politically, economically, socially and culturally over a generation, so that we can begin to co-ordinate our short-term decisions as far as possible to contribute towards movement in the desired direction. This is no abstract academic luxury. It is central to the quality of our future performance. It is an integral part of catering for the needs of the family, for instance, about which we purport to be so concerned, because it is vital for the future of our children. Strategy must identify where we are, why we are here, where we want to go, and how to get there.

Strategic thinking obliges us to confront the reality that our current condition is not merely the result of a once-for-all misguided deviation from normalcy. If it were, it could be cured by a once-for-all return to normalcy, however painful the prescription. A strategic approach, however, compels us to recognise that our fundamental predicament is that our long-term economic performance since Independence has been unimpressive by comparative European criteria. No other economy in the whole of Europe appears to have experienced remotely so slow a growth of its total gross national product in the twentieth century. [2] If we do not look quite so forlorn in terms of per capita income, that is because our population has grown more slowly than that of virtually any other European state in the past sixty years. [3] Even in terms of per capita income, however, we have fallen much further behind every other state, except Britain, that was ahead of us sixty years ago. In addition, we have fallen far behind every state that was abreast of us then. Every state then below us, whether in western or eastern Europe, from the Atlantic to the Urals, and from the Baltic to the Mediterranean, has either narrowed the gap significantly with us, or overtaken us. Our standard of living has, of course, risen since Independence. But it has risen far less than that of any other European country, except Britain. [4] That is the really distinguishing feature of our economic performance. We have, it is true, performed poorly enough on most fronts in the past decade. But then so have many other European countries. In the short term, we are simply an extreme version of the general European case. But our longer-term performance cannot be described in those terms. It is simply sub-European.

Nor does it suffice to respond that even if we compare badly with virtually every other European country, we have nevertheless performed creditably compared with other 'new nations' of the twentieth century. That is largely false analogy. We were a unique 'new nation'. No other 'new nation' inherited so politically, economically or educationally advanced a legacy. To compare with other 'new nations' is in most respects both historically inaccurate and emotionally self-indulgent.

It is vital for purposes of national strategy to ponder the correct perspective on our performance. If we believe, for instance, that we have not done too badly, then we are unlikely to acknowledge the need to do much better. And we have done very badly, even in purely economic terms. We failed to achieve the average European growth rate for any sustained period since Independence. We lifted our game briefly in the 1960s, it is true, but even in the 1960s we did not reach the western European average, impressive though our performance may have been by our own earlier standards. And the seeds of the rotten harvest were already being sown from the late 1960s. We had an average annual inflation rate of more than 10% during the four years before the oil crisis of 1973. The oil crisis exacerbated our problems. But it did not create them. Both our unemployment and inflation rates were well above the European average before the crisis struck. And much of the artificial growth of the late 1970s was bought at the direct expense of the depression of the early 1980s. If there is one lesson that even the most reluctant amongst us should have taken to heart by now, it must be that we cannot return to the 1970s. That particular primrose path ought never to be trodden again. The real challenge that confronts us, however, is not so much to surmount a short-term crisis, necessary though that may be, but to achieve a new trajectory of long-term national performance.

It seemed as if we had come close to achieving that trajectory during the 1960s, as we escaped from the smog of depression that enveloped us in the 1950s. And there may be a temptation to hope for as dramatic an improvement in the late 1980s as occurred in the late 1950s. We surmounted a major economic and psychological challenge then. Why not now? It is a seductive analogy. But I fear it may be a false one. For we have arrived at our present position in a manner that leaves us worse equipped to confront the challenge. It is not only that the government has much less fiancial scope for manoeuvre than thirty years ago, thanks to our insistence on incurring a massive foreign debt in the intervening period. The situation has become more daunting for at least four other reasons. First, international circumstances are now generally less favourable. We cannot do much about that. Second, we have pursued an industrialisation policy that has left us dangerously dependent on foreign investment. The repatriation of profits by foreign firms equals about half our total income tax, and while the multinationals have widened the range of our export markets, and reduced our dependence on the British buyer, they have seriously increased our dependence on American decision-making, whether at governmental or company level. However genuine Irish-American friendship may be, it is always a mistake for a small country to allow itself become too heavily dependent on the goodwill of any other single state, particularly an incomparably more powerful one. The foreign investment policy was correct up to a point, but that point has now been well passed. Third, the Northern Ireland situation has become much more volatile and dangerous.

Most ominously of all, because it is the consequence of our own behaviour, government is now much weaker than thirty years ago. This may seem strange, for government has grown enormously. [5]

But size has not brought strength. Government is like a stranded whale. It is weaker than ever before in relation to vested interests and pressure groups in both the private and the public sectors. Lemass and Whitaker were able to impose their authority to a considerable extent on the public service. But the structure of government has now become far more complex. The number of officials in the higher grades of the civil service increased faster during the 1970s than in the whole previous history of the state. [6] Between 1960 and 1980, no fewer than forty-seven new state sponsored bodies were established. Some have served a purpose. But the expansion occurred in a hit or miss sort of way. It was nobody's business to think about an overall framework. We therefore now have a jerrybuilt institutional structure, fostering a whole cluster of formidably obstructive vested interests that impede effective decision-making. In so far as the surge of the 1960s can be attributed to policy, it was due to the impact of a fairly small number of able and patriotic individuals. When they departed, the systems did not prove resilient enough to sustain the momentum. The growth in the size of the public service brought more a deterioration than an improvement in decision-making capacities. The result is that it has become more difficult for even determined and clear-sighted leaders, whether politicians or administrators, to slice their way through the intestinal intricacies of the institutional maze.

The bigger government has grown, the more vulnerable it has become to the voracious demands of special interests. A luxuriant crop of pressure groups sprouted in the congenial conditions of the 1960s and 1970s. Older pressure groups became more aggressive. There was nothing unique to Ireland about this development. Something similar happened in most European countries. [7] But Ireland suffered disproportionately for several reasons. Our political system, in particular, failed conspicuously to develop in a manner capable of containing the predatory passions of the pressure groups, or of guarding the authority of the state from usurpation. The non-ideological, catch-all nature of the two main parties, which left both appealing to the total electorate, and therefore slow to take a stand against any pressure group, inordinately exposed the party system to extortionate demands.

Interest groups have a legitimate and constructive rôle to play in modern society. Indeed, it is difficult to see how a modern democratic state could operate without their contribution. But their influence has been increasingly exerted against the national interest as those with sufficient organisational muscle to seek continuing to live beyond the country's means have striven to force others to pay for their gains. This damaged the country's competitiveness, generated unemployment in the more exposed industrial sectors, and fostered a selfishness and cynicism that further corroded the sense of the public interest. It is now in the interest of the vast majority of the citizens, in anything but the shortest of short terms, that the state asserts its authority by at least snipping, if not chopping, the filching fingers of pressure group leaders. That requires political as well as administrative reform. Many of our best politicians are themselves prisoners of the electoral system. Previous efforts to change the system were so nakedly opportunistic that they were rightly rejected by the public. There is no perfect electoral system, and our present arrangements probably served the public interest better than any alternative for the first half century of Independence or so. It may now be time to consider again the 'Norton Amendment' of 1968, which unavailingly proposed the creation of single member constituencies with the single transferrable vote. Our unfortunate experience of government during the intervening period certainly suggests that improvement should be possible.

Improvement to what purpose? Strategic thinking has to focus on targets. Otherwise we evade the discipline of criteria and accountability. We could, for instance, set ourselves the target of reaching the average western European standard of living over the next twenty-five years, and measure our performance *en route* according to how close we were coming to the goal. Only by assessing ourselves against that criterion can we keep in perspective the inevitable short-term fluctuations. Without a target of that type, we are in danger of being lulled once more into complacency, or even into mindless optimism, by fortuitously favourable short-term developments in the international economy.

In one sense, that may seem a modest ambition. It does not demand that we strive to feature among the European front runners even a generation from now. In another sense, the goal may seem highly ambitious. It would require a level of sustained growth significantly higher than the western European average over the period. If we have never succeeded in surpassing the average for even a few years, how can we possibly expect to exceed it, on trend, over twenty-five years? It is precisely, however, because the gap between our potential and our performance is so wide that it should be possible to accelerate the comparative rate of growth. But if we are to shift the trajectory of national performance, we must play to our strengths. Our greatest potential strength lies in our people. We are a naturally intelligent, quick, good humoured people. Many individual Irish men and women perform brilliantly in their own spheres. But we seem unable to translate our individual talent into an impressive collective performance. We manage ourselves badly. That is the crucial bottleneck that has to be smashed by a strategy of national development.

If our collective performance lags so far behind our individual potential, it is in our institutional structures we must seek the explanation in the first instance. We have cobbled together fragmented institutional structures that hinder effective decision-making. We have also devised structures within institutions that foster widespread frustration. Many of our institutions seem to have brought to a fine art the pernicious knack of demotivating people. Many of our most worthwhile people are switched off, trapped within the system. The intensity, often self-defeating, with which we pursue wage and salary claims at least partly reflects this feeling of frustration. And I suspect that the initial public response to the Progressive Democrats, irrespective of that party's ultimate fate, suggests that it has tapped a deep vein of frustration among people who feel stifled by the existing systems, not only in politics but outside of it also, in which they feel condemned to pass their days.

Performance varies widely from person to person, according to attitude and aptitude, even within the same institutions. But structures are not neutral. They influence the behaviour of individuals to a considerable extent. They allow the more parasitic, or the more selfish elements, of which there are many, to drag down the more productive or the more patriotic, of which there are also many, to a lower level. Too many of our institutional structures, whether in the public or in the private sector, give a built-in advantage to the limpets, enabling them to thwart initiative behind a respectable facade. Few even of our best people are achieving their full potential.

Perhaps the most sustained thinking on the issue of how to get the best out of ourselves, how to organise our institutions — whether government departments, state-sponsored bodies, political parties, trade unions, private firms, educational bodies, the media, etc. — in such a way as to serve rather than subvert the essential national interest by unleashing the talent cooped up within them, is coming from some civil servants, originally stimulted by the Devlin Report of 1969, and recently encouraged, despite the resistance of vested interests, by the energy of the then Minister for the Public Service, John Boland, in forcing through a White Paper on administrative reform, *Serving the Country Better*. So primitive has been our level of intellectual activity, and so formidable the resentment and the inertia — the White Paper appeared seventeen years after the Devlin Report! — that this is the first policy document since Independence to grapple with the general quality of our decision-making in the public service. While the White Paper marks only a first step, and in some respects a tentative one, the condition of the country in twenty-five years' time will be more influenced by the success achieved in implementing its proposals, and in maintaining the impulse behind them, than by many other more stridently public initiatives. [8]

We have a big but weak state. A national strategy requires a smaller, but a stronger state, spending proportionately less, but spending it more effectively. The weakest sectors of society derive disproportionatley little benefit from the current public expenditure patterns. No people genuinely concerned with the plight of the deprived can countenance the present procedures for the allocation of resources. The current allocation has been 'nobbled' in many cases by sectoral interests directly subversive of the national interest. It often favours the muscle men of the society. In Irish circumstances the state has to be a major agent of national organisation. A leaner state does not mean a less active state in every area. On the contrary, there is a strong case for more state activity in some areas, and for less in others. A national strategy cannot afford an ideological approach to the rôle of the state, whether by left or right. We are increasingly importing, without reference to our historical circumstances, much of the jaded vocabulary of left-right political discourse in England. Both our public and our private sectors have such scope for improvement that we must encourage excellence in both. The only economic ideology a national strategy aiming to catch up with western Europe can countenance is the ideology of performance.

If public expenditure has become bloated, public administration has become centralised to a bizarre extent by European standards. It is not only the size, but the intense centralisation of government, that has fostered a dependency syndrome throughout our society. Dependency undermines self-respect and a sense of responsibility. Citizens cannot be expected to behave responsibly when they are given so little resposibility to exercise. Officials who genuinely deplore the intensity of public demands on the state are themselves responsible for reinforcing those demands through their craving for centralised power. Only through a systematic policy of decentralisation of decision-making authority, to regional and local level, can a sense of responsibility be fostered. Changes in mental attitudes are prerequisites for improving our national performance, but attitudes will not change as long as citizens are reduced to their present level of dependency on central government. Decentralisation solely on the basis of the existing authorities, however, with their plethora of rival competences and overlapping jurisdictions, with different boundaries applying for local authorities, IDA planning regions, health boards, tourist boards, educational committees, and so on, would make the present farcical situation even worse. We therefore need a coherent programme of decentralisation, along the lines proposed in the recent publication by Muintir na Tíre, *Towards a New Democracy*. A proper mayoral system, where lord mayors, as in most European countries, and in the United States, are elected by popular vote for a fixed term, so that the lines of local responsibility and accountability can be clear, should form an integral part of local government reform.

This is not a demand for extra layers of bureaucracy. That is the last thing Ireland needs. It is a demand for a fitter alternative to the present obese system of centralisation. It is a demand for less bureaucracy, not for more. It demands not supplementary layers to the present structure of government, but alternatives to it. To those who feel that even coherent decentralisation would be a recipe for chaos and corruption in our localist political culture, there are three responses. First, localism is normal in the most advanced western European societies. There can be few more localist societies anywhere than Switzerland, with much of its administrative power exercised by twenty-six cantons and no fewer than 3,029 districts (Gemeinden) in an area smaller than the twenty-six counties. But it has the highest standard of living in Europe, perhaps in the world. The difference is that *we* have hitherto devised systems that bring out much of the worst, and little of the best, in localist instincts. It is not so much our localism, as our failure to harness the potential of localism for community development, that distinguishes our administrative style. Second, critics of decentralisation imply that we now have a coherent administration. But in fact what we have is centralisation without cohesion. Despite the extreme centralisation, decision-making is both institutionally and intellectually fragmented. Rivalries are so intense within many government departments and semi-state institutions, much less between them, that to speak of co-ordinated government at present is to make a mockery of language. If the centralisers hold the locals to be unfit for self-government, the performance of centralised government has scarcely sufficed to silence the sceptics who hold the Irish to be unfit for self-government. Decentralisation might at least expose some of the sources of confusion, procrastination and evasiveness in our public administration, rather than concealing them behind the facade of centralisation. Third, a strategy of national development requires education in the concept of citizenship. The Swiss system could not work in Ireland. But that is not because the system cannot work. It is because the Irish cannot work it. It demands a level not only of organisational sophistication, but of civic consciousness, at present alien to Irish political and administrative culture. That is no reason to dismiss the idea of moving in that direction. Our civic culture will not remain frozen for ever. It has not descended from the mount on tablets of stone. Sixty-five years is a very short time span in the history of a people colonised for several centuries. It is unrealistic to expect mentalities moulded over a millenium to be sloughed off virtually over night. But a strategy of national development demands that we begin working consciously towards an alternative to the dependency syndrome. That can only come through more widespread participation in responsible local government. Of course mistakes will be made. But they will be made within a framework conducive towards movement in the right direction. Mistakes galore are made at present in central government where they are the price not of movement, but of malaise.

For a country that, like most small countries, has to rely so heavily on the quality of its thinking, we still invest extraordinarily haphazardly in systematic social thought. We do not think enough about how we ought to think. The first requirement for the development of a national strategy is a capacity to see ourselves in perspective. For a people reputedly obsessed with history, it is striking how little historical perspective we actually have, either on our own performance or that of others. We have devoted extraordinarily little attention to the systematic study of the history of Independent Ireland. The capacity to learn from one's own history, and from that of others, is itself a defining characteristic of advanced peoples. Only a small number of the world's peoples have mastered the art involved. We cannot yet fully count ourselves among them. We must begin to train ourselves to do some long-term thinking. Our short-term performance often depends on international circumstances beyond our control. But our long-term performance depends more on the quality of our own thinking, on our ability to detect underlying trends as distinct from surface manifestations, and on the correctness of the strategic response to those trends. It was precisely the lack of long-term perspective, historical and comparative, that contributed towards the sqandering of the initial achievement of T.K. Whitaker and Seán Lemass, when their policy of opening up the economy and importing the entrepreneurial talent so sadly missing at home helped to pull the country out of the debilitating depression of the 1950s and surge forward during the 1960s. We did not devise appropriate criteria to assess our own performance, and despite Whitaker's regular warnings [9] — we allowed ourselves to be dazzled by the glitter of increasingly superficial success, and we continued to pursue much the same industrial policy oblivious to the longer-term implications.

We have got the results our mindlessness deserves. The many other smaller European countries who have pulled so far ahead of us in this century do not enjoy superior natural resources. They simply organised their main resources, the intelligence of their people, more effectively. We ought to make it a high priority to closely study the mobilisation of intelligence in these societies to see how they organise and utilise their brain power. We need ideas desperately. But we have tried to get them at cut price. It is a false economy. We have numerous institutions, including universities and research institutes, concerned with bits and pieces of the thinking process. But nobody seems to be charged with responsibility for thinking strategically about the direction of national development. And strategic thinking is a technique that has to be learned. It does not actually require too much money. But it does require much thought. Flinging money mindlessly at badly defined problems not only does not solve the existing problems but actually creates fresh ones on top of them.

A national strategy requires a fundamental reassessment of the relationship between cultural change and economic change. We instinctively tend to segregate the two, treating the economic as a necessity and the cultural, in the broadest sense, as a luxury. That is an elementary but crucial mistake. Economic growth, even in the narrowest sense, cannot be explained in purely material terms. We are unique among the now sovereign states of Europe in having abandoned our language, reputedly to sell the cow. The irony is that other small states, who lacked the imagination to take so apparently progressive a step as jettisoning their obscure languages, have sold the cow distinctly more successfully than ourselves, literally and metaphorically. We bartered the language. But we could not even get a proper mess of pottage for it. The language is lost unless government fosters its revival through example. That seems unlikely to happen. The language will therefore become even more a museum piece, to be fleetingly and furtively exhibited on occasions of public ritual, a ghostly reminder of our unusual feat in losing on the cultural swings and losing on the economic roundabouts. From a purely material utilitarian viewpoint, the loss of the language, far from smoothing the path to economic development, has arguably proved a major handicap in emulating the standards of the other small states who have succeeded in mobilising their cultures to provide a motivation for economic development. If a sense of national identity is crucial, as I believe it to be, to creating co-operative rather than selfish mentalities, to fostering a commitment to consensus rather than conflict, then the loss of the language obliges us to work exceptionally hard at forging the type of mentality essential to sustain long-term collective achievement. Indeed, achieving that objective without the sense of identity conferred by possession of the historic language may seem an even more Utopian objective than the revival itself.

We import most of our ideas. That is inevitable for a small, English-speaking country. But the import of ideas is a highly skilled activity. We have no filter through which to sift inappropriate ideas because we have failed to develop a serious tradition of native social thought. And because of our immersion in the English-speaking world, we have imitated much, but learned little. We do not learn. We mimic. We must resolve as a society to begin learning systematically for the first time in our history. Michael Fogarty's reference earlier in this book to 'the lack of awareness of too many Irish managers of the standards of workmanship, management and general business leadership in the world outside' applies equally emphatically to many other areas of Irish life. There is no mystery about the process. The more successful small peoples do it consciously. But their decision-makers have normally mastered several languages, and have taken the elementary precaution of preserving their own, which enables them to import more selectively.

The social dangers inherent in a cultural vacuum can be detected from the manner in which we have embraced technology as the elixir of future growth. Technological change is indeed crucial to our future. But it is disturbing to see how we have characteristically snatched at 'high-tech' as yet one more quick fix. Technological policy, and the social consequences of technological change, require deep thought. But the country lacks the intellectual framework within which to situate serious thinking on the issue. Unless we can incorporate the rôle of technology into a national strategy, and simultaneously subordinate it to that national strategy, so that we become its masters rather than its servants, we will be inevitably baffled when technological change creates predictable problems that once again we have failed to anticipate.

We must draw the disturbing lessons of our patent failure over the past twenty-five years to foresee the impact of economic and technological change on the quality of life in the country in general, and in Dublin in particular. How Dublin copes with its problems is a national issue. We had the advantage of the late starter, in respect to the timing of our most rapid economic development. Yet we failed lamentably to learn from the earlier experience of others. One of the most important influences on the nature of family life, for instance, is where the family is located. We have the most sparsely populated inhabitable territory in western Europe. We ought to be able to avoid the worst social and residential consequences of urbanisation. Instead, we have insisted on packing an exceptionally high proportion of our population into a single conurbation, while simultaneously protesting our commitment to the values of family life. And there is no sign of change. The recent report of the Eastern Regional Development Organisation (ERDO), rejoicing in the title of a settlement strategy, contains little evidence of strategic thinking. [10] Instead, it seeks to impose a sectoral perspective — sectoral both geographically and technically — on society. It seems oblivious to the fact that we have already made life a waste land for many weaker elements in the capital, particularly for the old, many of whom suffer terrible loneliness and live in fear of the vandal and the criminal in precisely the type of urban environment that the ERDO Report seeks to perpetuate and even extend. A proper national strategy must repudiate the assumptions on which that Report is based. It is not the eruption of social problems that is puzzling, but our failure to anticipate them when they are in large measure the direct result of our misguided population settlement and urban planning policies.

The vast increase in educational expenditure in the past twenty-five years has left us more educated. Whether it has left us better educated is debatable. Too much of that education has arguably been a training in technique rather than an investment in thought. We are in danger of becoming a well-trained, badly educated people. We are not educating our young people for social change, because the fashionable thrust of educational policy is to train students to think more about things than about people. Perhaps the new Curriculum and Examinations Board at second level can exert some impact here. It has a considerable responsibility thrust upon it, and it will be instructive to see how it responds. It is handicapped precisely by the absence of a national strategy, which obliges it to operate within a fragmentary framework. We can predict that until the quality of strategic social thinking is raised, the country will continue to extract the worst rather than the best from technological change.

It is one of the ironies of technological advance that it makes the quality of social and moral thought more rather than less important. Warnings about the quality of our social thought could be shrugged off when it was assumed that economic growth automatically lifted all boats. That can no longer be assumed. Thinking about the social consequences of technological change has become even more important as it has become clear that growth no longer automatically creates jobs. But national strategy must make more provision for investment in social thought. Likewise, the basic values of a society become more important when technology enhances the range of choice open to that society.

The approach outlined in this paper may sound impractical to 'practical' men. But too many of our practical men have been proved highly impractical by the acid test — success or failure in the open market, whether it be the market for ideas or for goods. What is impractical is the attempt to cling to the present discredited systems, which have so patently failed to serve the national interest. It cannot be repeated too emphatically that, for no obvious reason, Ireland has failed sadly to achieve her potential even in the narrowly economic sphere to which so much else has been sacrificed. It is no accident that, in terms of both total gross national product and per capita income, we now compare far more poorly with the European average than we did at the time of Independence. If there is a mould to be broken in Irish life, it is the mould of collective mediocrity. Defenders of the status quo are in fact demanding a mandate for mediocrity.

The Economic and Social Research Institute was founded at one of the few moments in Irish history when a determined attempt was being made, if only by a handful of patriots, to think strategically. That moment passed all too quickly. But that attitude must now be recaptured if the next twenty-five years are to result in more sustained achievement than the last twenty-five. Even if most of the things that need to be done are done they will not bear full fruit for many years. Nevertheless, if the analysis of this paper is correct, no country in Europe (except perhaps Britain) could improve its performance so rapidly, because no people in Europe (except perhaps the British) is performing so far below its potential as ourselves. The challenge is to devise the mechanisms that will allow our more generous and constructive instincts to flourish. Otherwise we will continue plugging holes in the dyke while the waves come breaking over the top. If we choose to continue to search for the quick fix, to indulge the politics of the promiscuous promise, we will never come near to realising our own full potential as people, even if we are occasionally wafted upwards on the waves of international recovery. If we determine, however, to take responsibility for our own long-term development, then one may hope that the concluding lecturer in the Thomas Davis Series celebrating the fiftieth anniversary of The Economic and Social Research Institute, twenty-five years hence — if there is a twenty-five years hence, and over that we have little control in this nuclear age — will be able to look back on a quarter century that will at last have begun to fulfil the long-postponed promise of Independence. [11]

NOTES

2. Ireland in the World Economy
1. The front page of the *Wall Street Journal*, 5 November 1985, carried an article on GPA with the caption 'Small Irish Firm Leads Fast-Growing Market for Aircraft Leasing'.
2. Dr Whitaker drew attention to this in his essay (No. 1 in this volume).
3. Richard Williams of 'Euromoney' in *The Sunday Independent*, 24 February 1985.
4. P. Lynch, 'The Economics of Independence: Some Unsettled Questions of Irish Economics', *Administration*, vol. 7 no. 2, 1959.

3. Employment, Unemployment and Emigration.
1. John A. O'Brien (editor) *The Vanishing Irish*, McGraw-Hill, New York, 1953.

4. Industry: The Revolution Unfinished.
1. The nature and extent of the political transformation is examined in P. Bew and H. Patterson, *Seán Lemass and the Making of Modern Ireland 1945-1966*, Gill and Macmillan, Dublin, 1982.
2. For further discussion of the role of small manufacturing firms, see K.A. Kennedy and T. Healy, *Small-Scale Manufacturing Industry in Ireland*, The Economic and Social Research Institute, Dublin, 1985, Paper No. 125.
3. C. Cooper and N. Whelan, *Science, Technology and Industry in Ireland*, Report to the National Science Council, Stationery Office, Dublin, 1973.
4. For further details, see the masterly review of the literature by E. O'Malley in National Economic and Social Council, *Industrial Policy and Development: A Survey of Literature from the Early 1960s to the Present*, Report No. 56, Dublin, 1980.
5. There are wide differences of opinion on this point, however. The IDA would claim that it made every conceivable effort, and with considerable success, to attract projects with greater linkages and deeper roots. On the other hand, the Science Policy Research Centre stated, in regard to the Cooper and Whelan proposals, that 'the main recommendations of the report ... have yet to be implemented' — Science Policy Research Centre, University College, Dublin, *Suggestions on Policies for Science to the National Board for Science and Technology*, Dublin, 1978.
6. National Economic and Social Council, Dublin:
- *Industrial Policy and Development: A Survey of Literature from the Early 1960s to the Present*, Report No. 56, 1980;
- *The Importance of Infrastructure to Industrial Development in Ireland* — *Roads, Telecommunications and Water Supply*, Report No. 59, 1981;
- *A Review of Industrial Policy*, Report No. 64 (popularly known as the Telesis Report), 1982;
- *Policies for Industrial Development: Conclusions and Recommendations*, Report No. 66, 1982;
- *An Analysis of Job Losses in Irish Manufacturing Industry*, Report No. 67, 1983; and
- *The Role of the Financial System in Financing the Traded Sectors*, Report No. 76, 1984.

7. National Economic and Social Council, *The Role of the Financial System in Financing the Traded Sectors,* Report No. 76, Dublin, 1984.

8. D. McAleese, 'Industrial Policy and Performance in Ireland' paper presented to the Conference on *A Competitive Strategy for European Sunrise Industries* held in Erasmus Universiteit, Rotterdam, 18-20 September 1985.

5. Agriculture and other Natural Resources.

Bibliography

Bórd na Móna, *Developing Ireland's Peat Resources,* Dublin, David Cailot, (editor), *The State of the Environment,* An Fóras Forbartha, Dublin, 1985.

Denis Conniffe and Kieran A. Kennedy (editors), *Employment and Unemployment Policy for Ireland,* The Economic and Social Research Institute, Dublin, 1984, Chapters 10 and 11.

Martin J. Cranley, 'The Natural Resources of Ireland', *Administration,* Vol.24, No.1, 1976.

Donal Daly, 'Ground Water Quality and Pollution', *Information Circular 85/1,* Geological Survey of Ireland, 1985.

Department of Energy, *Energy in Ireland,* Stationery Office, Dublin. 1983.

W.K. Downey and G. Ní Uid, *Air Pollution: Impact and Control,* Proceedings of a Seminar, Galway, National Board for Science and Technology, 1978.

P.P.R. Gardiner, A.M. Flegg, P. McArdle and J.P. Pyne, 'A Summary of Ireland's Mineral Resources' *Information Circular 84/1,* Geological Survey of Ireland, 1984.

Robert Kane, *The Industrial Resources of Ireland,* 2nd Edition, Hodges and Smith, Dublin, 1845.

National Economic and Social Council, *Irish Forestry Policy,* Report No. 46, Dublin, 1979.

National Economic and Social Council, *Minerals Policy,* Report No. 60, Dublin, 1981.

National Economic and Social Council, *Irish Energy Policy,* Report No. 74, Dublin, 1983.

R. O'Connor, 'The Current Agricultural Situation', *The Irish Banking Review,* June 1981.

R. O'Connor, 'The Irish Sea Fishing Industry', *Allied Irish Bank Review,* July 1981.

R. O'Connor, C. Guiomard and J. Devereux, *A Review of the Common Agricultural Policy and the Implications of Modified Systems for Ireland,* Broadsheet No. 21, The Economic and Social Research Institute, Dublin, 1983.

S.J. Sheehy, 'The Impact of EEC Membership on Irish Agriculture', *Journal of Agricultural Economics,* Vol. XXXI, No. 3, September 1980.

Water Pollution Advisory Council, 'A Review of Water Pollution in Ireland', *Report to the Council,* An Fóras Forbartha, Dublin, June 1983.

6. The Growth of Government.

Humphreys, Peter C. *Public Service Employment: An Examination of Strategies in Ireland and Other European Countries,* Dublin: Institute of Public Administration, 1983. OECD, *The Role of the Public Sector: Causes and Consequences of the Growth of Government.* OECD, Paris (Special Issue of OECD *Economic Studies,* No.4, Spring 1985).

7. Living Standards.

References

John Blackwell, 'Government, Economy and Society' in F. Litton (ed.) *Unequal Achievement,* Institute of Public Administration, Dublin, 1982.

Economic Development, Stationery Office, Dublin, 1958. First Programme for Economic Expansion, Stationery Office, Dublin, 1958.

Brian Girvin, 'Industrialisation and the Irish Working Class since 1922', *Saothar* 10, *Journal of the Irish Labour History Society,* Dublin, 1984.

Kieran A. Kennedy and Brendan R. Dowling, *Economic Growth in Ireland: The Experience since 1947,* Gill and Macmillan, (in association with the ESRI), Dublin 1975.

Patrick Lynch, 'Whither Science Policy?' *Administration,* Vol. 27, No. 3, 1979.

NIEC Report No. 18, *Full Employment,* Stationery Office, Dublin 1967.

NESC Report No. 55, *Urbanisation: Problems of Growth and Decay in Dublin,* Stationery Office, Dublin, 1981.

NESC Report N. 64, *A Review of Industrial Policy,* Stationery Office, Dublin, 1982.

NESC Report No. 65, *Farm Incomes,* Stationery Office, Dublin, 1982.

David B. Rottman and Damian F. Hannan, 'Fiscal Welfare and Inflation: Winners and Losers' in *The Irish Economy and Society in the 1980s,* Proceedings of 21st Anniversary Conference, The Economic and Social Research Institute, Dublin, 1981.

David B. Rottman, Damian F. Hannan, Niamh Hardiman and Miriam M. Wiley, *The Distribution of Income in the Republic of Ireland: A Study in Social Class and Family Cycle Inequalities,* The Economic and Social Research Institute, Dublin, 1982.

David B. Rottman, Damian F. Hannan, and Niamh Hardiman, Miriam M. Wiley, Litton (ed.) *Unequal Achievement,* Institute of Public Administration, Dublin 1982.

Second Programme for Economic Expansion, Stationery Office, Dublin, 1964.

Christopher T. Whelan and Brendan J. Whelan, *Social Mobility in the Republic of Ireland: A Comparative Perspective.* The Economic and Social Research Institute, Dublin, 1984.

8. Class and Social Mobility.

1. John H. Goldthorpe, *Social Mobility and Class Structure in Modern Britain,* Clarendon Press, 1980, p. 39.

2. Howard Rosenbrock, 'Engineers and The Work That People Do', in Craig R. Littler (ed.), *The Experience of Work,* Gower, 1985, p. 162.

3. Anthony Giddens, *The Class Structure of Advanced Societies,* Hutchinson, 1973, pp 131-132.

4. C.T. Whelan and B.J. Whelan, 'Adjustment to Retirement: Economic and Social Influences' in Public Social Expenditure — Value for Money? The Economic and Social Research Institute. 1984a.

5. R. Sennett and J. Cobb, *The Hidden Injuries of Class,* Vintage Books, 1973.

6. Anthony Giddens, op. cit., p. 131.

7. David B. Rottman, Damian F. Hannan and Niamh Hardiman, Miriam M. Wiley, *The Distribution of Income in the Republic of Ireland: A Study in Social Class and Family Cycle Inequalities,* The Economic and Social Research Institute, Paper No. 109, 1982.

8. David B. Rottman and Philip J. O'Connell, "The Changing Social Structure", in F. Litton (ed.) *Unequal Achievement,* Institute of Public Administration, Dublin, 1982, p. 71.

9. White Paper on Educational Development, 1980, Stationery Office, Dublin, 1980, p. 6.3. and National Economic and Social Council, *Irish Social Policies: Priorities for Development,* Report No. 61, Dublin, 1981, para. 2.11.

10. Christopher T. Whelan and Brendan J. Whelan, *Social Mobility in the Republic of Ireland: A Comparative Perspective,* The Economic and Social Research Institute, Paper No. 116, Dublin, 1984b pp., 38-42 and 104-117.

11. Anthony Heath, *Social Mobility,* Fontana, 1981, p. 57.

12. Whelan and Whelan, 1984b, op. cit.

13. Ibid, pp. 74-79 and pp. 117-128.

14. Ibid, pp. 137-139.

15. Damian F. Hannan, Richard Breen and Barbara Murray, Dorothy Watson, Niamh Hardiman, Kathleen O'Higgins, *Schooling and Sex Roles: Sex Differences in Subject Provision and Student Choice in Irish Post-Primary Schools,* The Economic and Social Research Institute, Paper No. 113, Dublin, 1983, p. 53.

16. Whelan and Whelan (1984b) op. cit., p. 157.

17. Richard Breen, 'Irish Educational Policy: Past Performance and Future Prospects', in *Public Social Expenditure — Value for Money?,* The Economic and Social Research Institute, 1984a, p. 105.

18. A.H. Halsey, 'Towards Meritocracy; The Case of Britain' in J. Karabel and A.H. Halsey (eds.) *Power and Ideology in Education,* Oxford University Press, 1977.

19. Richard Breen, *Education and the Labour Market: Work and Unemployment Among Recent Cohorts of Irish School Leavers,* The Economic and Social Research Institute, Dublin, Paper No. 119, 1984b, pp. 78-95.

20. Ibid, pp. 79-83.

21. Ibid., pp. 122-127.

22. Terry Corcoran, 'Irish Youth Employment Policies in the 1980s', *Administration,* Vol. 33, No. 2, 1985, pp. 262-263.

23. V. Greaney and T. Kellaghan, *Equality of Opportunity In Irish Schools,* The Educational Company, 1984.

24. Department of Education, *Programme for Action in Education,* 1984, 3.1, 3.3 and 5.5.

25. Breen (1984 b), op. cit., 102.

26. Adrian Raftery and Michael Hout, 'Does Irish Education Approach the Meritocratic Ideal? A Logistic Analysis', *The Economic and Social Review,* Vol. 16, No. 2, 1985, p. 139.

27. Breen (1984a) pp. 45-46.

28. Whelan and Whelan (1984b), pp. 163-175, Raftery and Hout (1985).

29. Hannan and Breen, *et al.,* 1983, op. cit., pp. 88.92.

30. Damian F. Hannan and Maura Boyle,*The Differentiation of Pupils and Curricula in Irish Second-Level Schools,* The Economic and Social Research Institute, forthcoming.

31. Christopher T. Whelan, *Worker Priorities, Trust in Management and Prospects for Workers' Participation,* The Economic and Social Research Institute, Paper No. 111, Dublin, 1982, p. 59.

9. The Family in Transition

1. Many people helped me in the preparation of this essay. Professor Kieran A. Kennedy, Professor Patrick Lynch and Professor Gary Becker gave both comment and encouragement. Kieran F. and Ruth Kennedy made some acute observations on content as well as suggestions on style. I am very grateful to all who helped and in particular to Michael Littleton who shared the fruits of his vast experience in broadcasting and to M. McElhone who saw the paper through publication.

2. C. M. Arensberg and S. Kimball, *Family and Community in Ireland,* Harvard, 1940.

3. Alexander Humphreys, *New Dubliners: Urbanisation and the Irish Family,* Routledge and Kegan Paul, London, 1966.

4. Damian Hannan, *Rural Exodus. A study of the forces influencing the large-scale migration of Irish rural youth,* Geoffrey Chapman (Ireland), 1970.

5. *op. cit.,* p. 121.

6. James F. Meenan, *The Irish Economy Since 1922,* Liverpool University Press, 1970.

7. *op. cit.*, p. 337.
8. Brendan Walsh, 'Ireland's Demographic Transformation, 1958-1970', *The Economic and Social Review*, Vol. 3, No. 2, 1972.
9. Gary Becker. *A Treatise on the Family*, Harvard, 1981, p. 244.

Selected References

J. Harold Abramson, *Issues in Adoption in Ireland*, The Economic and Social Research Institute, Dublin 1984.
C. M. Arensberg and S. Kimball, *Family and Community in Ireland*, Harvard, 1940.
Gary Becker, *A Treatise on the Family*, Harvard, 1981.
Gary Becker, 'Human Capital, Effort and the Sexual Division of Labor', *Journal of Labour Economics*, Vol. 3, No. 1, 1985.
Terence Browne, *Ireland, A Social and Cultural History, 1922-1979*, Fontana Paperbacks, 1981.
Family Studies Unit, *The Changing Family*, University College, Dublin, 1984.
R.C. Geary, 'The Family in the Irish Census of Population', *Journal of the Statistical and Social Inquiry Society of Ireland*, Vol. 19, 1954/55.
Damian Hannan, *Rural Exodus. A study of the forces influencing the large-scale migration of Irish rural youth*, Geoffrey Chapman (Ireland), 1970.
- 'Kinship, Neighbourhood and Social Change in Irish Rural Communities', *The Economic and Social Review*, Vol. 3, No. 2., 1972.
- and Louise Katsiaouni. *Traditional Families? From Culturally Prescribed to Negotiated roles in Farm Families*, The Economic and Social Research Institute, Dublin, 1977.
Alexander Humphreys, *New Dubliners: Urbanisation and the Irish Family*, London, Routledge and Kegan Paul, 1966.
James Meenan, *The Irish Economy Since 1922*, Liverpool University Press, 1970.
Reports of the Commission on Emigration and Other Population Problems, Dublin, Stationery Office, 1954.
Valerie Richardson, *Whose Children?* University College, Dublin, 1985.
Brendan Walsh, 'Ireland's Demographic Transformation 1958-1970', *The Economic and Social Review*, Vol. 3, No. 2, 1972.
Working Party on Women's Affairs and Family Law Reform. *Irish Women: Agenda for Practical Action*, Dublin, Stationery Office, 1985.

10. Crime and the Criminal Justice System
1. This description of recent Irish crime trends is a summary of the material from a number of research studies and monographs, especially Rottman (1977, 1980, 1985) and Breen and Rottman (1985).
2. Summaries of the available evidence on offender characteristics can be found in the Council for Social Welfare (1983) and Rottman (1985, Appendix 1).
3. I have argued in various research studies that Irish crime statistics are routinely misused by the mass media, politicians, and pressure groups in whose interest it is to show that crime has risen or fallen. Any claim that attributes importance to the difference between the crime statistics in two adjacent years should be discounted. Crime statistics can indicate long-term shifts in the level and seriousness of offences, and even that only if they are used selectively. This requires specific offence categories that are well-defined, likely to be reported to the gardaí, and indicative of both the amount and the nature of criminal activity in the community. Homicide, robbery, and burglary are examples of suitable indicators; minor property offences, such as larceny or vandalism, are not. The standard measure — the total number of indict-

able offences — is meaningless as a measure of crime, containing an arbitrary mixture of offences ranging from murder to public mischief, each assigned equal importance.

4. Crime victimisation surveys complement rather than supplant official crime statistics. The latter provide the only enumeration of offences which has been 'screened' to be certain complaints match the legal specifications for when an offence has been committed. For discussions of the alternative merits of surveys and official crime statistics, see Hough and Mayhew (1983) or Breen and Rottman (1985). English figures are from Hough (1984) and Irish figures from unpublished results of the ESRI Crime Victimisation Survey.

5. More detailed discussions of change in the legal system can be found in Casey (1982), Boyle and Greer (1984), and McMahon (1985).

6. The Conroy Report was followed by a succession of other reports on the garda siochána: The Ó Briain Report (on conditions of custody) and the Ryan Committee, as well as the unpublished report by management consultants Stokes, Kennedy and Crowley. In 1985, yet another committee, with a mandate to examine Garda training, was established. McDowell (1964) provides a brief but authoritative description of the RIC, while Brady (1974) is the standard reference on the Garda Síochána.

7. The basis for the term 'discovery' is the account given by McMahon (1985) of developments in the 1960s.

8. Sociologists such as Poggi (1978, pp. 101-149) argue that the very existence of industrial democratic society depends on the state's strict adherence to the rule of law in all of its decisions. To do otherwise threatens the 'legitimacy' of the social order, the belief by citizens that compliance with authority is right and obligatory rather than something we do for our personal gain or out of fear.

9. There are no reliable routinely collected statistics on court outcomes in this country. In consequence, public opinion is largely shaped by the cases reported in the mass media. Those cases are selected for mention because they are atypical and thus a distorted picture of conviction rates and sentencing severity or consistency has emerged. The most detailed picture of how cases are actually processed in the Irish criminal courts can be found in Rottman and Tormey (1985). See also Robinson (1974) and Needham (1983).

10. This argument is based on Bryan Wilson's (1985, p. 331) thesis that 'rational organisation has reduced the function of morality', with the modern era bringing 'not so much a change *in* morality or of the extent of its application, as a change *from* morality to an alternative underpinning of social order'. An essay by Liam Ryan (1984) offers an interpretation of the Irish experience over recent decades.

11. The distinction between criminal opportunity and criminal motivation is useful but artificial. It is perhaps easier to be law-abiding in a situation where a scarcity of consumer goods offers little in the way of temptation to disobedience. Also, the growth of contractual-type relationships increased the contact individuals have with large, impersonal organisations. This change provided new opportunities for crime and a new type of victim — e.g., a corporation or government department which by their very scale and abstract character are perhaps regarded as more acceptable targets by potential criminals.

12. The evidence for this assertion is various ESRI studies summarised by Whelan (1985).

13. The possibilities are critically reviewed in McCullagh (1985).

14. Quoted in Mannheim (1965, p. 422).

References
Conor Brady, *Guardians of the Peace*, Dublin: Gill and Macmillan, 1974.
Richard Breen and David Rottman, *Crime Victimisation in the Republic of Ireland*. Dublin: The Economic and Social Research Institute, Report No. 121, 1985.

C.K. Boyle and D.S. Greer, *The Legal Systems, North and South*. Dublin: Stationery Office (A Study Prepared for the New Ireland Forum), 1984.

James Casey, 'Law and the Legal System 1957-82' in F. Litton (ed.) *Unequal Achievement: The Irish Experience 1957-82*. Dublin: Institute of Public Administration, 1982.

COMMISSION ON THE GARDA SÍOCHÁNA, *Report on Remuneration and Conditions of Service* (the Conroy Report). Dublin: Stationery Office, 1970.

Committee to recommend certain safeguards for persons in custody and for members of an Garda Síochána, *Report* (The Ó Briain Committee). Dublin: Stationery Office, 1978.

COMMITTEE OF INQUIRY INTO THE PENAL SYSTEM, *Report* (the Whitaker Report), Dublin: Stationery Office, 1985.

COUNCIL FOR SOCIAL WELFARE, *The Prison System*. Dublin, 1983.

GARDA SÍOCHÁNA COMMITTEE OF INQUIRY, *Report*. Dublin: Stationery Office, 1979.

Mike Hough, 'Residential Burglary: a Profile from the British Crime Survey' in R. Clarke and T. Hope (eds.) *Coping with Burglary*. Boston: Kivwes-Nijhoff, 1984.

Mike Hough and Pat Mayhew, *The British Crime Survey: First Report*. London: HMSO (Home Office Research Study No. 76), 1983.

J.J. Lee, 'Continuity and Change in Ireland, 1945-70' in J.J. Lee (ed.) *Ireland:1945-70*. Dublin: Gill and Macmillan, 1979.

Ciaran McCullagh, 'Community Policing: a Critique of Recent Proposals', *The Economic and Social Review*, Vol. 16 April, 1985.

R.B. McDowell, *The Irish Administration: 1801-1914*. London: Routledge and Kegan Paul, 1964.

Bryan M.E. McMahon, 'A sense of identity in the Irish legal system' in J.J. Lee (ed.) *Ireland: Towards a Sense of Place*. Cork: Cork University Press, 1985.

Hermann Mannheim, *Comparative Criminology*. Boston: Houghton Mifflin, 1965.

Michael Needham, *The District Court — An Empirical Study of Criminal Jurisdiction*. LL.M. Thesis, University College Galway, 1983.

Gianfranco Poggi, *The Development of the Modern State: A Sociological Introduction*. Stanford: Standford Univerity Press, 1978.

Mary Robinson, *The Special Criminal Court*. Dublin: Dublin University Press, 1974.

David Rottman, 'Crime and Law Enforcement' in *Towards A Social Report,* Dublin: National Economic and Social Council, Report No. 25, 1977.

David Rottman, *Crime in the Republic of Ireland: Statistical Trends and Their Interpretation,* Dublin: The Economic and Social Research Institute, Report No. 102, 1980.

David Rottman, *The Criminal Justice System: Policy and Performance*. Dublin: National Economic and Social Council, Report No. 77, 1985.

David Rottman and Philip Tormey, 'The System in Criminal Justice' in *Public Social Expenditure — Value for Money?* Dublin: The Economic and Social Research Institute, 1984.

David Rottman and Philip Tormey, 'The Criminal Justice System: An Overview' in *Report of the Committee of Inquiry into the Penal System* (Part 2, Section 2). Dublin: Stationery Office, 1985.

Liam Ryan, 'The Changing Face of Irish Values' in *Irish Values and Attitudes: The Irish Report of the European Value Systems Study*. Dublin: Dominican Publications, 1984.

Christopher T. Whelan, *'Class and Social Mobility'*, in this volume.

Bryan R. Wilson, 'Morality in the Evolution of the Modern Social System'. *British Journal of Sociology,* Vol. 36 September, 1985.

11. The Two Faces of Irish Industrial Relations.

Select bibliography

C. Carter and J. Pinder, *Policies for a Constrained Economy,* Heinemann, 1982.
Commission of Inquiry on Industrial Relations, *Report,* Stationery Office, Dublin, 1981.
M. Costello, *Ireland's Experiment with Worker Directors,* Institute of Personnel Management, Dublin, 1983.
Department of Labour Discussion Document on 'Industrial Relations Reforms in Ireland', November 1983.
M.P. Fogarty, *Irish Entrepreneurs Speak for Themselves,* The Economic and Social Research Institute, Dublin, Broadsheet No. 8, 1973.
M.P. Fogarty, 'The Irish Economy — An Outside View' in *The Economic and Social State of the Nation,* a series of public lectures to mark the twenty-first anniversary of the ESRI, Dublin, 1982.
M.P. Fogarty, *Report on Banks Inquiry,* Stationery Office, Dublin, 1971.
M.P. Fogarty, (Chairman) *Final Report of the Committee on Industrial Relations in the Electricity Supply Board,* Stationery Office, Dublin, 1969.
M.P. Fogarty, L. Ryan and J. Lee, *Irish Values and Attitudes,* Dominican Press, Dublin, 1984.
M.P. Fogarty, D. Egan and W.J.L. Ryan, *Pay Policy for the 1980s,* Federated Union of Employers, Dublin, 1981.
M.P. Fogarty, D. Egan and W.J.L. Ryan, *Work-Sharing,* Federated Union of Employers, Dublin, 1984.
M.P. Fogarty, D. Egan and W.J.L. Ryan, *Clearing the Road to Employment,* Federated Union of Employers, Dublin, 1985.
M.P. Fogarty, 'Industrial Relations in AnCO', unpublished confidential report, 1977.
M.P. Fogarty, 'Industrial Relations in RTE', unpublished confidential report, 1978.
L. Gorman and E. Molloy, *People, Jobs and Organisations,* Irish Productivity Centre, Dublin, 1972.
B. Hillery, A. Kelly and A. Marsh, *Trade Union Organisation in Ireland,* Irish Productivity Centre, 1975.
Industrial Democracy in Europe International Research Group, *Industrial Democracy in Europe,* Oxford, 1980.
Industrial Democracy in Europe International Research Group, *European Industrial Relations,* Oxford, 1981.
Irish Marketing Services, 'Findings on Public and Trade Unionists' Reaction to Compulsory Strike Ballots and Reference of Disputes to the Labour Court', *FUE Bulletin,* August/September 1985.
W.E.J. McCarthy, J.F. O'Brien and V.G. Dowd, *Wage Inflation and Wage Leadership,* Paper No. 79, The Economic and Social Research Institute, Dublin, 1975.
D. Nevin, 'Industry and Labour' in K.B. Nowlan and T.D. Williams (eds.) *Ireland in the War Years and After,* Gill and Macmillan, Dublin, 1969.
D. Nevin (ed.) *Trade Unions and Change in Irish Society,* Thomas Davis Lectures, Mercier, 1980.
J.F. O'Brien, *A Study of National Wage Agreements in Ireland,* Paper No. 104, The Economic and Social Research Institute, Dublin, 1980.
L. Ryan (ed.) *Industrial Relations in Ireland — Is There a Case for Reform?* Helicon Press, Dublin 1984.

12. The Regional Dimension.

1. W.L. Micks, *History of the Congested Districts Board,* Dublin, 1925.

2. For a lively discussion see Riccardo Petrella, *The Demands of the Periphery,* European Co-operation Fund, Brussels, 1977 . See also P. Cooke, *Theories of Planning and Spatial Development* London, 1983 .

3. Significantly, the 'Social' dimension was not present in the original title of either the NIEC or the ERI. The authority charged with Gaeltacht development, *Údarás na Gaeltachta,* while it has responsibilities appropriate to a regional development agency, is better considered as an authority *sui generis* because of the linguistic imperatives which apply in the full range of its economic and social activities. For a useful discussion of this problem see Colin H. Williams, *Language Planning, Marginality and Regional Development in the Irish Gaeltacht* (Discussion Paper in Geolinguistics. No. 10 North Staffordshire Polytechnic, 1985).

4. The main sources for this summary are Hughes (1975) and the essay by M. Ross in Dowling and Durkan (1978), cited in the reading list.

5. The relevant literature is cited in P.N. O'Farrell (1975) and Helen B. O'Neill (1971).

6. Cited in *IDA Industrial Plan 1977-80,* p. 37.

7. This is hinted at in M. Ross and B. Walsh (1979), and in the essay by L. Ryan 'Development — The Role of the Community', in D. Ó Cearbhaill (1981).

8. *White Paper on National Development 1977-80,* (in the section on 'Industrial Development').

9. This point is made forcefully by Joseph Lee in Joseph Lee (editor), *Ireland: Towards a Sense of Place* (Cork, University Press, 1985).

10. S.J. Sheehy and R. O'Connor, *Economics of Irish Agriculture* (Institute of Public Administration, Dublin 1985). I am grateful to my colleague, Professor Michael Cuddy, for permitting me to consult his paper *The Performance of Irish Agriculture in its First Decade under CAP,* prior to its publication.

11. See, for example, B.M. Brunt, 'Manufacturing changes in the Greater Cork Area 1980-1984', in *Irish Geography,* 17, 1984.

12. This, of course, raises serious questions about the extent to which the ratio or multiplier of non-manufacturing to manufacturing jobs can be considered region-specific.

13. Cited by T. Barrington in his essay in F. Litton (1982), pp. 89 et seq.

14. ibid., p. 106.

15. The division of the greater Dublin area into new administrative and electoral units in 1985 is too recent to allow for any evaluation of its consequences. For a stimulating set of new proposals for local government reform see the recent *Towards a New Democracy,* published in 1985 by *Muintir na Tíre.*

16. Patrick Clancy, *Participation in Higher Education* (1982); the government's opening proposals on regionalisation in education were announced in December 1985.

17. See the report of the Eastern Region Development Organisation, *Eastern Region Settlement Strategy — 2011* (Dublin, 1985). For another perspective on regional growth see *Development Strategy to 2004* (West Region Study, prepared for the West Regional Development Organisation and the Commission of the European Communities, Dublin 1983).

18. It should be pointed out, as the editor of this volume properly reminded me, that the costs and benefits of decentralisation are different when one is starting from scratch from what they are when a considerable build-up of investment and infrastructure has already taken place in a particular area. This, of course, makes the task of identifying the costs and benefits of any proposed measure of decentralisation

more difficult and more urgent.
19. Brian Farrell (editor), *Communications and Community in Ireland* (Mercier, Dublin & Cork, 1984); also, Martin McLoone and John MacMahon (editors), *Television and Irish Society* (Radio Telefís Éireann/ Irish Film Institure, 1984).

Reading List

1. M.J. Bannon, J.G. Eustace and M. O'Neill, *Urbanisation: Problems of Growth and Decay in Dublin.* NESC, Report No. 55 Dublin, 1981.
2. M.J. Bannon, J.G. Eustace and Mary Power, *Service-type employmenmt and Regional Development,* NESC, Report, No. 28, Dublin 1977.
3. J. Barrington, *From Big Government to Local Government: The Road to Decentralisation,* IPA, Dublin, 1975.
4. H.C. Bos, *Spatial Dispersion of Economic Activity,* Rotterdam University Press, 1965.
5. L.S Bourne, R. Sinclair and K. Dzienwonski (editors), *Urbanisation and Settlement Systems,* Oxford, University Press, 1983.
6. Patrick Clancy, *Participation in Higher Education — A National Survey,* The Higher Education Authority, Dublin, 1982.
7. B.R. Dowling and J. Durkan (editors), *Irish Economic Policy: A Review of Major Issues,* The Economic and Social Research Institute, Dublin, 1978.
8. Norman J. Gibson and John E. Spencer (editors), *Economic Activity in Ireland,* Gill and Macmillan, Dublin 1977.
9. J.G. Hughes, *Regional Policy in Ireland: A Review,* NESC, Report No. 4, Dublin 1975.
10. Industrial Development Authority, *Industrial Plan 1977-80,* Dublin, 1978.
11. O. Katsiaouni, *A Pilot Study of Regional and Community Development in the Mid-West,* IPA, Dublin, 1975.
12. Frank Litton (editor), *Unequal Achievement: The Irish Experience 1957-1982,* IPA, Dublin, 1982.
13. G. Myrdal, *Economic Theory and Underdeveloped Regions,* Duckworth, London, 1957.
14. Diarmaid Ó Cearbhaill (editor), Full Employment and Regional Development: Issues and Policies, Officina Typographica, Galway, 1981.
15. P.N. O'Farrell, *Regional Industrial Development Trends in Ireland 1960-1973,* IDA Dublin, 1975.
16. Helen B. O'Neill, *Spacial Planning in the Small Economy: A Case Study of Ireland,* Praeger, New York and London, 1971.
17. *Programme for National Development 1978-1981* (White Paper), 1979.
18. M. Ross and B. Walsh, *Regional Policy and the Full-Employment Target,* The Economic and Social Research Institute, Dublin, 1979.
19. *Eastern Region Settlement Strategy — 2011,* Eastern Regional Development Organisation, Dublin, 1985.

13. The Church and Change.

1. Dogmatic Constitution on the Church *(Lumen Gentium). Vatican Council II: The Conciliar and Post-Conciliar Documents,* Dominican Publications (1975), ed. Austin Flannery, OP, Chapter IV, Paragraph 31, page 389.
2. Decree on the Ministry and Life of Priests *(Presbyterorum Ordinis)* ibid. Chapter II, Paragraph 9, Page 880.

14. Politics and Change.

1. For a fuller discussion see B. Farrell, 'The Unlikely Marriage: de Valera, Lemass and the Shaping of Modern Ireland'. *Etudes Irlandaises,* forthcoming 1986.
2. Michael Gallagher, 'Societal Change and Party Adaptation in the Republic of

Ireland', *European Journal of Political Research,* 9, 3, Sept. 1983, p.273.

3. Cf. Tom Garvin, 'The Growth of Faction in the Fianna Fáil Party, 1966-80' *Parliamentary Affairs,* XXXIV, 1, Winter 1981.

4. Cf. New Ireland Forum, *Report,* Stationery Office, Dublin, 1984.

5. Terence Brown, *Ireland: a Social and Cultural History 1922-79,* Fontana, London 1981, p. 282.

6. Tom Garvin, 'Change and the Political System', in F. Litton, ed., *Unequal Achievement : the Irish Experience, 1957-1982,* Institute of Public Administration, Dublin, 1982, p. 32. For references on the 'constitutional crusade' see B. Farrell, 'The Context of Three Elections', in H. Penniman and B. Farrell, (eds.) *Ireland at the Polls 1981—1982, A Study of Three General Elections,* American Enterprise Institute, Washington D.C., forthcoming 1986.

7. David M. Farrell, 'Age, Education and Occupational Backgrounds of TDs and "Routes" to the Dáil : the effects of localism in the 1980s', *Administration,* 32, 3, 1984, p. 330. See also M. Gallagher, '166 Who Rule : the Dáil Deputies of November 1982', *The Economic and Social Review,* 15, 4, 1984.

8. Cf. B. Farrell, 'Ireland : from friends and neighbours to clients and partisans; some dimensions of parliamentary representation under PR-stv', in V. Bogdanor, (ed.), *Representatives of the People? Parliamentarians and constituents in Western democracies,* Gower for Policy Studies Institute, London 1985.

9. The seminal article is John H. Whyte, 'Ireland : Politics Without Social Bases', in R. Rose (ed.), *Electoral Behaviour: a comparative handbook,* Free Press, New York, 1974.

10. Richard Sinnott, 'The Voters, the Issues and the Party System', in Penniman and Farrell, *op. cit.*

11. Michael Marsh, 'Electoral Volatililty in the Republic of Ireland, 1948-83', in Ivor Crewe and David Denver, (eds.), *Electoral Volatility in Western Democracies,* Croom Helm, London 1984.

12. Gallagher, *op. cit.,* p. 273.

13. Cf. David M. Farrell, 'The Strategy to Market Fine Gael in 1981', Michael Laver and Paul Arthur, eds. *Irish Political Studies Yearbook 1986,* forthcoming 1986.

14. J.J. Lee, 'Sean Lemass', in J.J. Lee, (ed.), *Ireland 1945-70,* Gill and Macmillan, Dublin, 1979, p. 20.

15. T.J. Barrington, 'Whatever happened to Irish government', in F. Litton, *op. cit.,* p. 104. See also Basil Chubb, 'Prospects for democratic politics in Ireland', in Penniman and Farrell, *op. cit.*

16. New Ireland Forum, *The Cost of Violence Arising from the Northern Ireland Crisis since 1969,* Stationery Office, Dublin 1983.

17. Public opinion polls have consistently shown that economic issues are regarded as considerably more important than the North by the vast majority of respondents.

18. Chubb, *op. cit.*

19. Cf. B. Farrell, 'Government Formation and Ministerial Selection', in Penniman and Farrell, *op. cit.*

15. Whither Ireland? The Next Twenty-Five Years!

1. For a rueful reminder by an eminent social scientist of the fallibility of forecasting at the macro level, see E.K. Scheuch, 'Aus Fehlprognosen Lernen', *Der Monat,* n.f., 297, 1985, pp. 235-239.

2. P. Bairoch, 'Europe's Gross National Product: 1800-1975', *Journal of European Economic History,* 5, 2, Fall 1976, p. 304.

3. Basic data on the earlier period can be found in B.R. Mitchell, *European Historical Statistics 1750-1970,* Macmillan, London, 1975, pp. 19 ff.

4. For relevant figures before 1970 see P. Bairoch, 'The Main Trends in National Economic Disparities Since the Industrial Revolution' in P. Bairoch and M. Lèvy-Leboyer (eds.), *Disparities in Economic Development Since the Industrial Revolution,* Macmillan, Basingstoke, 1981, p. 10. For later figures see OECD, *Annual Economic Surveys.*

5. B. Chubb, *The Government and Politics of Ireland,* Longman, London, 1982, 2nd ed., p. 256.

6. Ibid.

7. There is a voluminous literature. See in particular S. Berger (ed.) *Organising Interests in Western Europe,* Cambridge Univeristy Press, Cambridge, 1981, and J.H. Goldthorpe (ed.), *Order and Conflict in Contemporary Capitalism,* Clarendon Press, Oxford, 1984.

8. For various responses to the White Paper see T.J. Barrington, 'Serve you Right?', *Administration,* 33, 4, 1985, pp. 431-434, and the whole issue of *Seirbhis Phoibli,* 6, 4, Samhain 1985.

9. The melancholy story of the ignoring of the warnings can be followed in T.K. Whitaker, *Interests,* Institute of Public Administration, Dublin, 1983.

10. Eastern Regional Development Organsiation, *Eastern Regional Settlement Strategy 2011,* Eastern Regional Development Organisation, Dublin, 1985.

11. The thinking in this essay has been much influenced by the series *Ireland in the Year 2000* under the aegis of An Fóras Fórbartha and the NBST Dublin, 1980, and by L. Wrigley, 'Ireland in Economic Space', in Joseph Lee (ed.), *Ireland: Towards a Sense of Place,* Cork University Press, Cork, 1985, pp. 66-83. I am grateful to Kieran Kennedy for timely criticism. The usual disclaimer applies.

Milestones in Irish History

Edited by Liam de Paor

Milestones in Irish History spans the whole range of time from early prehistory to the present, opening with Frank Mitchell's enquiry into the social and historical meaning of the building of the remarkable cemetery of megalithic tombs centred on the great monuments of Knowth, Dowth and Newgrange. Liam de Paor looks at the background and work of St Patrick; Donnchadh Ó Corráin deals with Brian Boru and the Battle of Clontarf and Michael Richter examines the advent of the Normans.

Margaret MacCurtain discusses the Flight of the Earls and this is balanced, as it were, by an investigation of the new order that was created in its place in Aidan Clarke's look at the Plantations of Ulster. The Act of Union which made Ireland part of the United Kingdom in 1801 is examined by James McGuire and Kevin B. Nowlan looks at the career of Daniel O'Connell and Catholic Emancipation.

R. B. Walsh traces the decline of the Irish language and Donal McCartney examines the efforts to revive it at the turn of the century. Joseph Lee analyses the long drawn out struggle over the possession of land and Ronan Fanning gives his views on the partitioning of Ireland. John A. Murphy concludes with a look at the meaning of Ireland's entry to the EEC.

The Course of Irish History
Edited by T. W. Moody and F. X. Martin

Though many specialist books on Irish history have appeared in the past fifty years, there have been few general works broadly narrating and interpreting the course of Irish history as a whole, in the light of new research. That is what this book, first published in 1967, set out to do; and it is a measure of its success that it is still in demand, being now in its sixteenth printing.

The first of its kind in its field, the book provides a rapid short survey, with a geographical introduction, of the whole course of Ireland's history. Based on the series of television programmes first transmitted by Radio Telefís Éireann from January to June 1966, it is designed to be both popular and authoritative, concise but comprehensive, highly selective but balanced and fair-minded, critical but constructive and sympathetic. A distinctive feature is its wealth of illustrations.

The present edition is a revised and enlarged version of the original book. A new chapter has been added, bringing the narrative to the end of 1982, and the illustrations have been correspondingly augmented. The list of books for further reading has been expanded into a comprehensive bibliography of modern writings on Irish history. The chronology has been rewritten, updated, and much enlarged, so that it now amounts to a substantial supplement to the text. Finally, the index has been revised and extended both to include the new chapter and to fill gaps in the original coverage.

The book has been planned and edited by the late Dr T. W. Moody, fellow emeritus and formerly professor of modern history, Trinity College, Dublin, and Dr F. X. Martin O.S.A., professor of medieval history, University College, Dublin – an appropriate partnership for this enterprise of scholarly cooperation. Of the other 19 contributors, 17 are or were on the staffs of the universities and university colleges of Ireland and two were on those of the universities of Cambridge and of Manchester.

Leaders and Workers

Edited by J. W. Boyle

Here are portraits of nine men (William Thompson, John Doherty, Feargus O'Connor, Bronterre O'Brien, James Fintan Lalor, Michael Davitt, William Walker, James Connolly, James Larkin) whose lives between them span a century and a half, linking the days of the United Irishmen with our own. They include a forerunner of Marx, Chartists, trade union pioneers, champions of tenant farmers' and women's rights, leaders in the Irish and British labour movements. Though they came from different backgrounds, each of them, whether reformer or revolutionary, thinker or socialist – and some filled most of these roles – desired, like Thomas Russell, to alter conditions in which property was put before life. Even the least successful gave their followers in bleak and bitter times a fresh sense of human dignity and informed them with some of their own passion for the creation of a society freed from inequality and injustice. It is this passion that makes the lives and ideas of these nine Irishmen of continuing interest today.

Contributors: Patrick Lynch, Andrew Boyd, Asa Briggs, Thomas P. O'Neill, T. W. Moody, J. W. Boyle, Desmond Ryan, James Plunket

Michael Collins and the Treaty
His Differences with de Valera

T. Ryle Dwyer

To Michael Collins the signing of the Treaty between Ireland and Britain in 1921 was a 'Stepping Stone'. Eamon de Valera called it 'Treason'.

The controversy surrounding this Treaty is probably the most important single factor in the history of this country, not only because it led to the Civil War of 1922-1923 but also because the basic differences between the country's two main political parties stem from the dispute.

T. Ryle Dwyer not only takes an in-depth look at the characters and motivations of the two main Irish protagonists but also gives many insights into the views and ideas of the other people involved on both sides of the Irish Sea.

This book is not only the story of Michael Collins' role in the events surrounding the Treaty, but it is also the story of his differences with Eamon de Valera which were to have tragic consequences for the nation.

De Valera's Darkest Hour, 1919-1932

T. Ryle Dwyer

De Valera's Darkest Hour is the story of Eamon de Valera's struggle for national independence during the most controversial period of his career. It deals with his election as Priomh Aire of Dáil Éireann, his unauthorised assumption of the title of President, his controversial tour of the United States, his obscure part in the negotiations leading to the Anglo-Irish Treaty and his reasons for rejecting the Treaty. De Valera's misunderstood rôle in the period leading up to and during the Civil War, and finally his spectacular recovery in lifting himself from the despised depths of 1923 to become President of the Executive Council of the Irish Free State in less than nine years are covered in detail.

De Valera's Finest Hour, 1932-1959

T. Ryle Dwyer

Throughout his long career de Valera was a controversial figure but his greatest critics give him credit for his courageous denunciation of international aggression during the 1930s and for his adroit diplomatic skill in keeping Ireland out of the Second World War in the face of Nazi provocation and intense Allied pressure. His policy was guided by one paramount consideration – his concept of the best interests of the Irish people. He pursued those interests with such determination that he became the virtual personification of Irish independence.

Dr Dwyer gives a graphic account· of de Valera's quest for independence. Of particular interest are well-chosen and carefully documented extracts from contemporary letters, speeches, newspaper articles, etc., giving many new insights into the thoughts and motives of this enigmatic politician, who has left an indelible imprint on Irish history.

The Years of the Great Test, 1926-1939
Edited by Francis MacManus

Twelve well-known writers give separate accounts of the years 1926-1939 in Ireland – a period just after the Irish Free State had been established and showing how men new to government dealt with problems that affected not only Ireland but the world.

The authors deal with social life, education, politics, literature, external associations, north-south relations. They survey the many aspects of life in the new Ireland with a real depth of understanding that should make an immediate appeal to those who are now benefiting from the seeds then sown.

'In the practical business of surviving, in developing new communities abroad, in assisting the sick and poor, also in avoiding extreme disparities in social relationships, that generation did not do too badly. It was certainly a good deal less spoilt than the present one.'   *T. Desmond Williams*

Contributors: T. Barrington, Vincent Grogan, David Kennedy, F. S. L. Lyons, Francis MacManus, Nicholas Mansergh, J. L. McCracken, James Meenan, Donal Nevin, Kevin B. Nowlan, Seán Ó Catháin SJ, David Thornley, Terence de Vere, T. Desmond Williams.